B EDITIONS

...min Franklin
...ist and Statesman
...ernard Cohen

•

...aurent Lavoisier
...and Revolutionary
...nry Guerlac

•

...lerk Maxwell
...Natural Philosopher
...F. Everitt

DS

Benja
Scient
I. B

Antoine-I
Chemist
He

James C
Physicist and
C.W

ANTOINE-LAURENT LAVOISIER
Chemist and Revolutionary

Henry Guerlac
Professor of the History of Science
Department of History
Cornell University

Illustrated with photographs

CHARLES SCRIBNER'S SONS
New York

Publisher's Note

DSB Editions constitute a series of books developed from articles in the *Dictionary of Scientific Biography*. Each is a biography of a major scientist.

The *Dictionary of Scientific Biography,* published by Charles Scribner's Sons under the sponsorship of the American Council of Learned Societies, was designed to provide reliable information on the history of science through articles on the professional lives of scientists. It covers all periods from classical antiquity to modern times but does not include careers of living persons. In many instances the articles represent either the first or the most important study yet made of an individual's body of work. The authors are professional historians of science or professionals in a particular scientific area who also take a scholarly interest in the past. The aim was to include scientific figures whose contributions made an identifiable difference to knowledge as a whole. Each article concludes with a bibliography that guides the reader to the original scientific works and to biographical sources covering personal and public life. Some articles also contain reference notes.

DSB Editions contain the complete contents of the original article, plus a preface by the author, a section of illustrations, and an index. The texts have been revised by the authors and in some cases expanded to add further personal data, and the bibliographies have been brought up to date when necessary.

Contents

Preface

Because this work was originally written for a dictionary devoted to the accomplishments of scientists, the emphasis was placed upon Lavoisier's scientific work as viewed in the light of the most recent scholarship. Those who wish to explore further Lavoisier's role as social reformer, financier, and as a participant in the early events of the French Revolution should consult the bibliography. .

There is a vast secondary literature on Lavoisier, yet so far as I am aware no extensive bibliography of significant books and articles about Lavoisier has ever been published: nothing, at all events, to compare with Duveen and Klickstein's *Bibliography of the Works of Antoine Laurent Lavoisier*. The bibliography in the present book, while making no pretense at completeness, may help fill that gap; I have tried to include all important publications through 1973. It is based on a more ambitious preliminary listing which I prepared under a grant from the National Science Foundation with the assistance of Professors Carleton Perrin and Leslie Burlingame. This mimeographed bibliography, which covers the years

1795 to 1968, is available in the History of Science Collections in the Olin Library at Cornell University.

I am glad to have this opportunity to thank those who assisted me directly and indirectly in the preparation of this work. For help in consulting the Lavoisier documents belonging to the Paris Academy of Sciences I am deeply indebted, as are all students of the history of French science, to the kindness of Mme. Pierre Gauja, who presides over the Academy's extensive archives. Count Guy de Chabrol was kind enough on two occasions to accord me the privilege of working with the Lavoisier manuscripts and letters in his possession. Professor Charles Gillispie, the editor of the *Dictionary of Scientific Biography,* was particularly patient and helpful in connection with the preparation of the original version. Deserving of special thanks are my ex-students Rhoda Rappaport, J. B. Gough, and Carleton Perrin, and my confrères in the history of science, Maurice Crosland, Robert Schofield, and William Smeaton, all of whom read early drafts and called my attention to errors of commission and omission. I am especially grateful to Maurice Daumas, Lucien Scheler, and Ellen Wells for assistance in assembling the illustrations, and to the members of the staff of the Olin Library at Cornell for their unfailing courtesy and ingenuity.

10

A Portfolio of Pictures

Antoine-Laurent Lavoisier. Engraved by Pierre Michel Alix from a painting by Jean François Garneray, a pupil of Jacques Louis David. Probably based on the David portrait of Lavoisier and his wife (page 31).

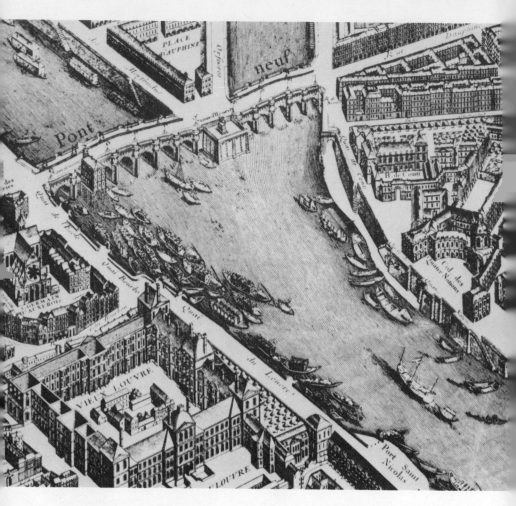

Portion of the Turgot plan of Paris (1739), showing the Old Louvre, where the Academy of Sciences met, and, across the river, the Collège des Quatre Nations, where Lavoisier was a student. This remarkable urban plan was commissioned by Michel Etienne Turgot, chief municipal official of Paris and father of the economist and philosophe Anne Robert Jacques Turgot.

Nicolas Louis de Lacaille, astronomer and teacher of Lavoisier at the Collège des Quatre Nations. Line engraving by Thérèse Devaux after a painting.

Jean-Etienne Guettard, Lavoisier's mentor in geology and mineralogy. This painting by Thomas Charpentier is the only known portrait of Guettard.

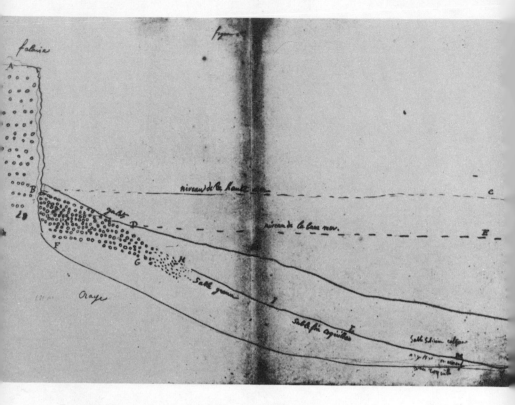

Lavoisier's preliminary sketch (ca. 1770) illustrating littoral or shoreline formations.

16

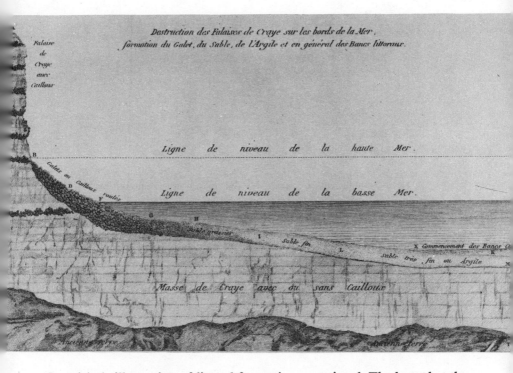

Lavoisier's illustration of littoral formations as printed. The legend at the top reads "Destruction of chalk cliffs at the seashore, formation of pebbles, sand, clay and in general of littoral formations." The cliff is labeled "chalk cliff with stones." The sea is shown as it appears in recent times, and the dotted line indicates the highest level reached in the past. The level below the sea shows the progression from pebbles through coarse sand, fine sand, and very fine sand or clay; at this point the beginning of a calcareous formation is shown. Below this sequence is a chalk mass "with or without stones," underneath which is the primitive formation that Lavoisier called the *"ancienne terre."*

17

A page of the field notes made by Lavoisier during an inspection tour of tobacco factories at Dunkirk (ca. 1770) in his capacity as traveling inspector for the General Farm, the tax-collecting body.

A symbolic testimony to the Abbé Rozier's contributions to agriculture. The bees, beehives, grapes, plows, milk cans, windmills, and other items suggest the topics treated in Rozier's twelve-volume *Cours complet d'agriculture.*

19

Pierre Joseph Macquer, the leading chemist of France in the generation before Lavoisier and author of a widely read dictionary of chemistry. Engraving by G. Benoist from a painting by J.P. Garrand.

Antoine Baumé, pharmacist and associate of Macquer, who remained faithful to the phlogiston theory. Drawn by Charles Nicolas
Cochin in 1772 and engraved by Augustin de Saint-Aubin.

Louis Bernard Guyton de Morveau, a lawyer and amateur chemist from Dijon. One of the earliest chemists to rally to the new chemistry of Lavoisier, he performed important experiments on the increase in weight of calcined metals and proposed a new chemical nomenclature. Drawn and engraved by Quenedey.

Jean Charles Philibert Trudaine de Montigny, public official and honorary member of the Academy of Sciences, with whom Lavoisier collaborated in some of his earliest experiments. Drawn by Charles Nicolas Cochin and engraved by Augustin de Saint-Aubin.

Pl·16·

p: 21

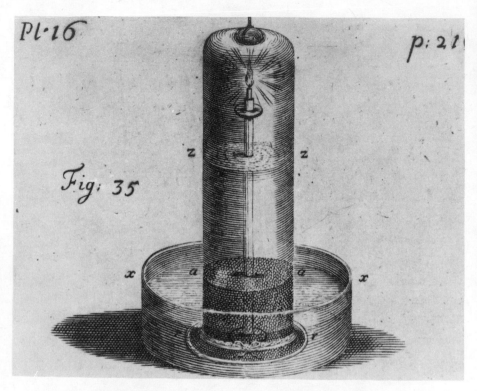

Fig: 35

Stephen Hale's pedestal apparatus for estimating the quantity of air absorbed or generated by a burning substance or by the breath of a living animal. A tall pedestal is placed in a basis of water. On the pedestal's platform Hales placed the candle, burning substance, or small animal; he "whelmed over it" an inverted glass *zzaa*, suspended by a cord so that its mouth *rr* was a few inches under water. With a siphon he drew air out of the glass vessel until the water level rose to *zz*. When air is absorbed, the water level rises; when it drops, it shows that air has been generated from the burning substance.

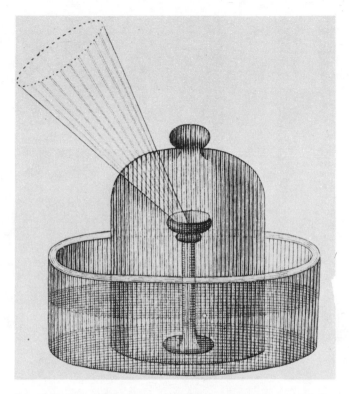

Lavoisier's modification of Hales's apparatus, used for studying the role of air in the calcination and reduction of metals. A bell jar is inverted over a pedestal of crystal in a basin of water. Water is drawn up to a certain level by means of a siphon, and a drop of oil is introduced under the bell jar, forming a film on the water surface to prevent any gas given off from being dissolved in the water. The substance to be ignited is placed in a crucible in the concave top of the pedestal and subjected to the heat of a burning glass. Lavoisier first used this apparatus in October 1772 to measure the air given off on the reduction of lead oxide. Drawn and engraved by Mme Lavoisier for her husband's posthumous *Mémoires de Chimie* (Paris, ca. 1805).

25

OPUSCULES
PHYSIQUES
ET CHYMIQUES,

Par M. LAVOISIER, de l'Académie Royale des Sciences.

TOME PREMIER.

A PARIS,

Chez
DURAND neveu, Libraire, rue Galande.
DIDOT le jeune, quai des Augustins.
ESPRIT, au Palais Royal.

M. DCC. LXXIV.

Title page of Lavoisier's first book. Only one volume was published.

Marie Anne Pierette Paulze, the future Mme Lavoisier, as a young girl. This engraving by Arents was made from a pastel portrait by an unkown artist.

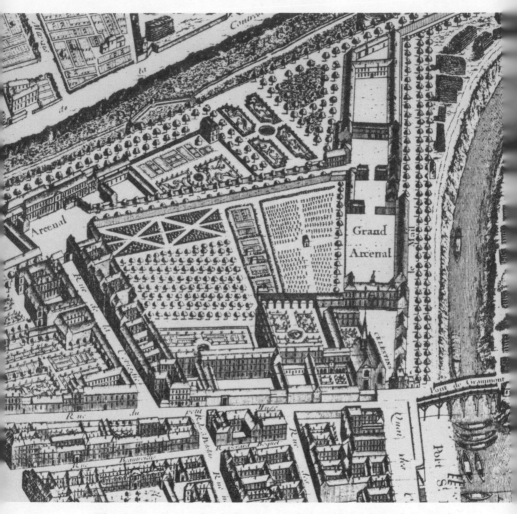

The Arsenal complex in Paris, consisting of the Grand Arsenal near the river and the Petit Arsenal (where Lavoisier is believed to have lived and worked from 1775 to 1792). The docking area (lower right) is the Port St. Paul, where cargoes to or from the Arsenal were handled.

The riot of the Arsenal. On 6 August 1789 a mob tried to prevent the transfer of gunpowder from the Paris Arsenal to warehouses at Essones, under the impression that Lavoisier and his colleagues wished to deprive Parisians of their arms. Actually, the directors merely wished to exchange the low-grade gunpowder in the Arsenal magazines for high-quality powder produced at Essones. Lavoisier barely escaped with his life. From a contemporary engraving.

29

Château de Fréchines
d'après une photographie.

Above: Lavoisier's country estate, the Château de Fréchines, where he carried out his chief agricultural experiments. It is located near the village of Ville-Francoeur in the old province of Orléanais (now the department of Loir-et-Cher).

Right: Lavoisier and his wife in about 1788. This painting by Jacques Louis David now hangs in the library of The Rockefeller University.

31

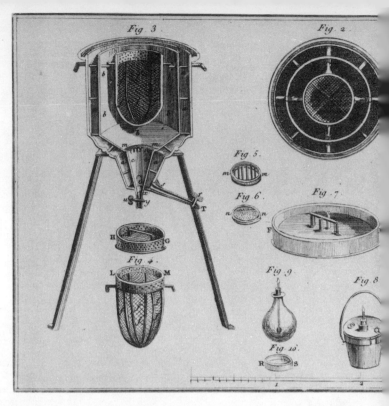

Above: The ice calorimeter of Laplace and Lavoisier, the earliest apparatus devised to measure the heat given off by a body, as distinct from measuring temperature. The heat produced is measured by the amount of ice melted. The exterior of the apparatus is shown in Fig. 1 and its cover in Fig. 7. Internally, as shown in Fig. 2, the calorimeter consists of three separate metal containers nesting one within another. In the vertical section (Fig. 3) the interior container *fffff* is a wire basket (also shown in Fig. 4) in which the experimental object is placed. The middle container *bbbbb* is for the ice melted by the experimental object; the ice is supported by a grill (Fig. 5), below which is placed a fine sieve (Fig. 6). The water from this melted ice flows down the cone *ccd* and the tube *xy* (with its stopcock *u*) and is caught in a vessel below (F in Fig. 1). The exterior container *aaaaaa* holds the ice which insulates the inner containers from the heat of the surrounding air; the runoff from this melting ice flows out the tube *sT*, which is provided with a stopcock *r*. Fig. 8 is an iron cannister to hold the materials to be experimented upon; its cover is pierced by a hole closed with a cork through which a fine thermometer is inserted. Fig. 9 is a glass vessel used when working with acids or other substances that act on metals, and Fig. 10 a small metal ring placed at the bottom of the inner container to support this vessel. Plate engraved by Mme Lavoisier for Lavoisier's *Traité élémentaire de chimie.*

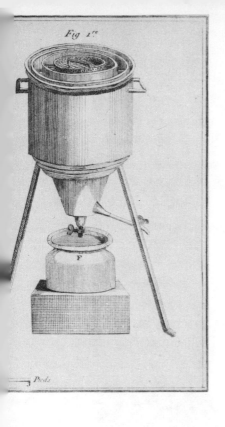

Below: Two surviving examples of the ice calorimeter now in the Musée des Techniques of the Conservatoire des Arts et Métiers, Paris. That on the left was adapted for experiments on the synthesis of water.

33

Gaspard Monge, painted by an unknown artist.

Pierre Simon Laplace. Unsigned engraving in the
Bibliothèque Nationale.

35

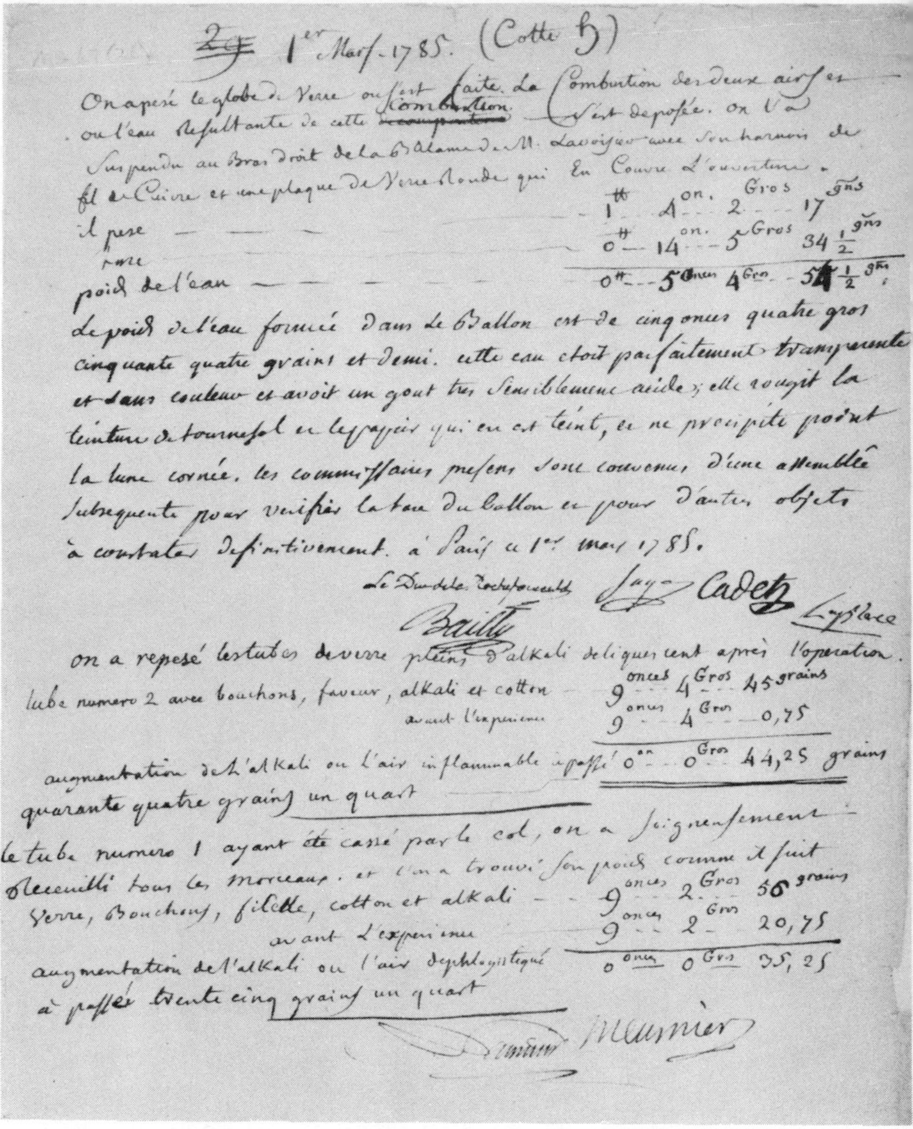

~~2~~ 1er Mars 1785. (Cotte h)

On a pesé le globe de verre où s'est faite la combustion des deux airs et où l'eau résultante de cette ~~décomposition~~ combustion s'est déposée. on l'a suspendu au bras droit de la balance de M. Lavoisier avec son harnois de fil de cuivre et une plaque de verre ronde qui en couvre l'ouverture.

il pese — 1# 4 on. 2 Gros 17 grains

vuide — 0# 14 on. 5 Gros 34 1/2 grains

poids de l'eau — 0# 5 onces 4 Gros 54 1/2 grains

le poids de l'eau formée dans le ballon est de cinq onces quatre gros cinquante quatre grains et demi. cette eau étoit parfaitement transparente et sans couleur et avoit un gout tres sensiblement acide; elle rougit la teinture de tournesol et le papier qui en est teint, et ne precipite point la lune cornée. les commissaires presens sont convenus d'une assemblée subsequente pour verifier la tare du ballon et pour d'autres objets à constater definitivement. à Paris ce 1er mars 1785.

Le Duc de la Rochefoucauld Sage Cadet Laplace

Bailly

on a repesé les tubes de verre pleins d'alkali deliquescent après l'operation.

tube numero 2 avec bouchons, faveur, alkali et cotton — 9 onces 4 Gros 45 grains

avant l'experience — 9 onces 4 Gros 0,75

augmentation de l'alkali ou l'air inflammable a passé — 0 on. 0 Gros 44,25 grains

quarante quatre grains un quart

le tube numero 1 ayant été cassé par le col, on a soigneusement recueilli tous les morceaux. et l'on a trouvé son poids comme il suit

verre, bouchons, ficelle, cotton et alkali — 9 onces 2 Gros 56 grains

avant l'experience — 9 onces 2 Gros 20,75

augmentation de l'alkali ou l'air dephlogistiqué — 0 onces 0 Gros 35,25

a passé trente cinq grains un quart

Lavoisier Meusnier

Record of an experiment for decomposing and synthesizing water on a large scale, signed by Lavoisier and Jean-Baptiste Meusnier and attested to by the Duc de la Rochefoucauld d'Enville, the chemists Sage and Cadet, the astronomer Bailly, and the mathematician Laplace.

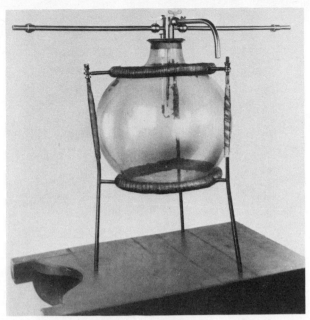

Top: Balloon flask for the synthesis of water, now in the Musée des Techniques of the Conservatoire des Arts et Métiers, Paris. The attached tubes bring together the hydrogen and oxygen gases.

Bottom: Large chemical balance built by Lavoisier's instrument maker, Nicolas Fortin, now in the collection of the Musée des Techniques of the Conservatoire des Arts et Métiers, Paris.

ESSAI

SUR

LE PHLOGISTIQUE,

ET SUR

LA CONSTITUTION DES ACIDES,

TRADUIT DE L'ANGLOIS DE M. KIRWAN;

AVEC DES NOTES

De MM. de Morveau, Lavoifier, de la Place,
Monge, Berthollet, & de Fourcroy.

A PARIS,

RUE ET HÔTEL SERPENTE.

1788.

Title page of the French edition of Richard Kirwan's *Essay on Phlogiston and the Constitution of Acids* (1784). The translation was made by Mme Lavoisier; the notes are by Lavoisier and his earliest disciples.

Joseph Priestley in 1791. Engraving by William Bromley.

Lavoisier's experiments on human respiration (1790-1791) with his collaborator, Armand Seguin. The drawings are by Mme Lavoisier, who shows herself taking notes at a nearby table. *Above:* the subject at rest; *opposite:* the subject performing work.

TRAITE
ÉLÉMENTAIRE
DE CHIMIE,

PRÉSENTÉ DANS UN ORDRE NOUVEAU

ET D'APRÈS LES DÉCOUVERTES MODERNES;

Avec Figures :

Par M. *LAVOISIER*, *de l'Académie des Sciences, de la Société Royale de Médecine, des Sociétés d'Agriculture de Paris & d'Orléans, de la Société Royale de Londres, de l'Institut de Bologne, de la Société Helvétique de Basle, de celles de Philadelphie, Harlem, Manchester, Padoue, &c.*

A PARIS,

Chez CUCHET, Libraire, rue & hôtel Serpente.

M. DCC. LXXXIX.

Sous le Privilège de l'Académie des Sciences & de la Société Royale de Médecine.

Title page of Lavoisier's best-known work, first edition, first issue, few copies of which are known.

Lavoisier during his imprisonment. Engraved by Mlle Brossard-Beaulieu from a drawing by an unknown artist.

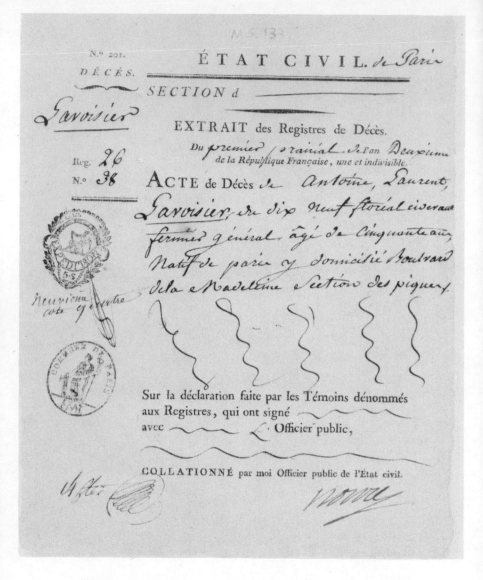

Certified copy, dated 1 Prairial An II (20 May 1794), of the official record of Lavoisier's death. It states that Antoine Laurent Lavoisier, one-time Farmer General, a native of Paris, domiciled Boulevard de la Madeleine, died at the age of fifty on 19 Floreal (8 April).

Antoine-Laurent Lavoisier
Chemist and Revolutionary

1. Family and Early Life

Remarkable for his versatility, as scientist and public servant, Lavoisier was first of all a chemist of genius, justly remembered for his discovery of the role of oxygen in chemical reactions and as the chief architect of a reform of chemistry, a reform so radical that he himself spoke of it early on as a "revolution" in that science. Yet Lavoisier also had a lifelong interest in geology and developed some original notions of stratigraphy; he was a pioneer in scientific agriculture, a financier of ability who holds a respected if minor place in the history of French economic thought, and a humanitarian and social reformer who used his position as a scientific statesman and landowner to alleviate the evils of society. His death on the guillotine in his fifty-first year, with creative powers still undiminished, has marked him, with the obvious exceptions of Louis XVI and Marie Antoinette, as the outstanding martyr to the excesses of the Reign of Terror during the French Revolution.

Lavoisier was a Parisian through and through and a child of the Enlightenment. Born in 1743, in the midreign of Louis XV and in the last year of the administration of Cardinal Fleury, his boyhood coincided with the flowering of the philosophic movement in France. The *Traité de dynamique*, which was to make d'Alembert's reputation, was published in the year of Lavoisier's birth. Voltaire's *Lettres philosophiques* had appeared ten years earlier (1733). Lavoisier was eight years old when the first volume of the *Encyclopédie* appeared and ten when Diderot, in his *Interprétation de la nature*, proclaimed that the future of science lay not in mathematical studies but in experimental physics—exemplified by the discoveries of Benjamin Franklin—and in chemistry.

Lavoisier's family, originally from Villers-Cotterets, a forest-encircled town some fifty miles north of Paris, was of humble, doubtless of peasant, origin.[1] His earliest recorded ancestor, a certain Antoine Lavoisier, was a courier of the royal postal service *(chevaucheur des écuries du roi)* who died in 1620; a son, another Antoine, rose to be master of the post at Villers-Cotterets, a position of some distinction. Three generations later Lavoisier's grandfather, still another Antoine, served as solicitor *(procureur)* at the bailiff's court of Villers-Cotterets and married Jeanne Waroquier, the daughter of a notary from nearby Pierrefonds. Their only son, Jean-Antoine, Lavoisier's father, was sent to Paris to study law. In 1741, still a mere fledgling in his profession, Jean-Antoine inherited the estate, as well as the *charge* of solicitor at the Parlement of Paris, of his uncle Jacques

Waroquier. The following year he married Émilie
Punctis, the well-dowered daughter of an attorney
(avocat) at the Paris law courts. Their first child,
Antoine-Laurent, the subject of this book, and a
younger sister who was to die in her teens, were both
born in the house in the cul-de-sac Pecquet (or
Pecquay) which had been the residence of the old
solicitor.[2] Here Lavoisier spent the first five years
of his life, until the death of his mother in 1748. This
bereavement led Jean-Antoine to move the two
children to the house of his recently widowed mother-
in-law, Mme Punctis, in the rue du Four near the
church of St. Eustache.[3] In this house, tenderly cared
for by an adoring maiden aunt, Mlle Constance
Punctis, Lavoisier passed his childhood, his school
days, and his young manhood until his marriage.

Lavoisier received his formal education in the
Collège des Quatre Nations, a remarkable school—
among its alumni were the physicist and mathematician d'Alembert, the astronomer J.-S. Bailly, and the
painter David—founded by the will of Cardinal
Mazarin and so commonly called the Collège Mazarin.
In the autumn of 1754, shortly after his eleventh
birthday, Lavoisier was enrolled as a day student
(externe) in the splendid building that today houses,
under its gilded dome, the constituent academies of
the Institut de France. At Mazarin, Lavoisier gained
a sound classical and literary training, earned more

than his share of literary prizes, and received the best scientific education available in any of the Paris schools. The course of study at Mazarin covered nine years; after the class of rhetoric, devoted to language and literature, and before the two years of philosophy, came a full year devoted to mathematics and the sciences under the tutelage of the distinguished astronomer Lacaille, famed for his expedition to the Cape of Good Hope and his charting of the stars of the southern hemisphere. We can gather something of Lacaille's teaching from his elementary books on mathematics, mechanics, optics, and astronomy. More than a trace of this training is to be found in Lavoisier's earliest scientific memoir, a highly precise description of an aurora borealis visible at Villers-Cotterets in October 1763. Observing it on a clear night, he showed his familiarity with Flamsteed's star table, carefully locating the streamers with respect to the visible stars and measuring their azimuth and altitude with a compass provided with an alidade.[4]

In 1761, rather than complete the class of philosophy leading to the baccalaureate of arts, Lavoisier transferred to the Faculty of Law; faithful, for the moment at least, to the family tradition, he received his baccalaureate in law in 1763 and his licentiate the following year.

Yet already his interest had turned to science, which he pursued in extracurricular fashion while carrying on his legal studies. Lavoisier may have received some further instruction from Lacaille in the intimacy of the latter's observatory at the Collège Mazarin, but only for a short while, for Lacaille died late in 1762. In the summer of 1763, and again the following year, Lavoisier accompanied the distinguished botanist Bernard de Jussieu on his *promenades philosophiques* in the Paris region.[5] Yet Jussieu's influence was probably slight—botany held little attraction for Lavoisier—whereas Lacaille's teaching helps account for Lavoisier's quantitative bent of mind, his lifelong interest in meteorological phenomena, and the barometric observations he made throughout his career.

Lavoisier's family and friends were soon aware that science had captivated the young man and was luring him away from the law. In an early letter (dated March 1762) Lavoisier was addressed by a family friend as "mon cher et aimable mathématicien"; and the same correspondent expressed concern that his young friend's health might suffer from his intense application to the various branches of science.[6] It is better, he continued—and Lavoisier would surely have disagreed—to have a year more on earth than a hundred years in the memory of men. Clearly, Lavoisier already displayed the boundless energy and wide-ranging curiosity that was to characterize him all his life; indeed another family friend, the geologist

Jean-Étienne Guettard, described him in these years as a young man whose "natural taste for the sciences leads him to want to know all of them before concentrating on one rather than another."[7] Yet it was Guettard who exerted the greatest influence upon Lavoisier and focused the young man's attention upon geology and mineralogy, and also, since it was an indispensable ancillary science, upon chemistry; for Guettard believed that to be "a mineralogist as enlightened as one can be," it was important to learn enough chemistry to be able to analyze, and so help to identify and classify, rocks and minerals.[8]

It was probably at Guettard's suggestion that Lavoisier attended the course in chemistry given by Guillaume–François Rouelle.[9] A brilliant and flamboyant lecturer and a vivid popularizer, Rouelle filled his lecture hall at the Jardin du Roi with a mixed audience of students, young apothecaries, society folk, and such well-known men of letters as Diderot, Rousseau, and the economist Turgot. Besides Lavoisier, the leading French chemists of at least two generations were introduced to the subject by Rouelle. Included in Rouelle's course was a series of lectures on mineralogical problems; besides describing the physical and chemical properties of mineral substances, Rouelle touched upon his own rather special theory of geological stratification.

Accordingly, persuaded that these lectures provided

the best—if not the only—instruction in mineralogy and the chemistry of minerals, Lavoisier followed them faithfully, probably in 1762–1763. If he attended the showy lectures at the Jardin du Roi, he almost certainly followed the private—and perhaps more technical—course Rouelle taught in his apothecary shop on the rue Jacob, near St. Germain des Prés.

2. Lavoisier as Geologist

Under Guettard's guidance geology had begun to absorb Lavoisier's attention. As early as 1763 he began his collection of rock and mineral specimens; and with Guettard he explored the region around Villers-Cotterets, where he was accustomed to vacation with relatives.

For some time, indeed since 1746, Guettard had nurtured a plan for a geologic and mineralogic atlas of France. It did not receive official support until 1766, when it was commissioned and funded by the royal government; but even earlier Guettard enlisted young Lavoisier as a collaborator. In repeated excursions in northern France—to Mézières and Sedan, through Normandy to the coast at Dieppe—the two men collected specimens, noted outcroppings, drew sections, and described the principal strata, assembling material for the atlas. Their intensive exploration and mappings continued until 1770, by which time they had completed and printed sixteen regional quadrangles, using symbols to designate the rock formations and mineral deposits.

The most extensive of these joint expeditions, and the most venturesome, was a trip through the Vosges

Mountains and parts of Alsace and Lorraine in 1767. Accompanied by Lavoisier's servant, Lavoisier and Guettard traveled on horseback for four months, often under trying, if not actually hazardous, conditions. The letters Lavoisier exchanged with his father and his adoring aunt during this long absence from Paris have largely survived; and Lavoisier's own warm, affectionate epistles are very nearly the only letters among the many extant in which we glimpse his personal feelings.

Lavoisier's special contribution to this venture, as to the other expeditions, was to add a quantitative character to their observations. He used the barometer systematically to measure the heights of mountains and the elevations and inclinations of strata, intending to use the results for drawing sections; and he collected samples of mineral and spring waters to be analyzed in the field or shipped back to Paris. Nor was all this deemed of purely practical value: by 1766 he had outlined a research program of experiments and observations that should lead him, in the language of the day, to a "theory of the earth," that is, to an understanding of the changes that had altered the surface of the globe.

For the most part, Lavoisier's early theories of stratification were derived from Guettard and Rouelle or from his reading of Buffon's *Théorie de la terre* of 1749. Guettard, of a largely practical turn of mind, described the geology of France in terms of three *bandes* differing in their lithology. Rouelle distinguished the *terre ancienne*, the granitic and schistose formations in which fossils apparently were absent, from the generally horizontal, sedimentary strata rich in fossils, which he called the *terre nouvelle*. The strata of the *terre nouvelle*, he believed, had been deposited when the sea covered all or most of the continent of Europe. Accepting Rouelle's division (although often using Guettard's terms), Lavoisier at first assumed that there had been only a single epoch in which the present continents were submerged. But he soon observed that the *terre nouvelle* was composed of two different kinds of strata: fine-grained, calcareous beds (pelagic beds), such as would result from a slow deposition in the open sea, and littoral deposits of rougher, abraded, and pebblelike material, formed at beaches and coastlines. These had been distinguished by his predecessors, but it was Lavoisier who noted that littoral and pelagic beds sometimes seemed to alternate with each other. As early as October 1766 he came to the radical conclusion—which greatly extended his conception of geologic time—that there may have been a succession of epochs marked by a cyclically advancing and retreating sea. In the regions he knew best there was not a single *terre nouvelle* but, rather, three different pelagic formations laid down at different times. Even the *terre ancienne* was not truly primitive rock; it was more likely, he remarked at one point, to be composed of littoral beds formed very long ago *(bancs littoraux beaucoup plus anciennement formés)*.

Lavoisier never lost interest in these geological problems, although after 1767 his opportunities for fieldwork markedly diminished; he continued, as far as innumerable distractions permitted, to be associated with the atlas project until 1777, the year when Antoine Monnet was officially put in charge of it. But it was not until 1788 that Lavoisier presented his theory of stratification to the Academy.

3. Scientific Début and the Academy of Sciences

Lavoisier's earliest chemical investigation, his study of gypsum, was mineralogical in character; begun in the autumn of 1764, it was intended as the first paper in a series devoted to the analysis of mineral substances. This systematic inventory was to be carried out, not by the method of J. H. Pott—who exposed minerals to the action of fire—but by reactions in solution, by the "wet way." "I have tried to copy nature," Lavoisier wrote. "Water, this almost universal solvent . . . is the chief agent she employs; it is also the one I have adopted in my work."[10] Using a hydrometer, he determined with care the solubility of different samples of gypsum (samples of selenite, or *lapis specularis*, some supplied by Guettard and Rouelle). He made similar measurements with calcined gypsum (plaster of Paris). Analysis convinced him that this gypsum was a neutral salt, a compound of vitriolic (sulfuric) acid and a calcareous or chalky base. Not content with having shown by analysis the composition of the gypsum, Lavoisier completed his proof by a synthesis following, as he said, the way that nature had formed the gypsum. He further demonstrated that gypsum, when transformed by strong heating into plaster of Paris, gives off a vapor, which he showed to be pure water, making up about a quarter of the weight of gypsum. Conversely, when plaster of Paris is mixed with water and turns into a solid mass, it avidly combines with water. Using the expression first coined by Rouelle, he called this the "water of crystallization."

This first paper, which in so many respects embodies the quantitative methods Lavoisier was to employ in his later work, had in fact been largely anticipated by others, notably by Marggraf, who had already discovered the composition of gypsum and shown that it contained water *(phlegm)*. Yet Lavoisier's work was more thorough; and his paper, his first contribution to the Academy of Sciences (read to the Academy on 25 February 1765), appeared in 1768 in what was usually called the *Mémoires des savants étrangers*, an Academy organ which published some of the papers read to that body by nonmembers, often by those who, like Lavoisier, aspired to membership.[11]

At the age of twenty-one Lavoisier was already an aspirant; to be sure, the time had passed when men of that tender age were readily admitted to the Academy as *élèves* or *adjoints*. Yet Lavoisier had friends in the Academy, and his father and his aunt were not averse to pulling such strings as came to hand. Meanwhile, the young man laid siege to the Academy from another angle. He resolved in 1764 to compete for the prize offered by the lieutenant general of police, and to be judged by the Academy, for the best method of improving the street lighting of Paris. The effort he put into this inquiry was prodigious; he attempted, as A. N. Meldrum put it, to exhaust the subject—theoretically, practically, and even (as he was to do so often in later inquiries) historically. He sought the best available material for lamp wicks and the combustible; he determined what shape—whether parabolic, hyperbolic, or elliptical—made the best reflectors; he recommended how lanterns should be suspended to give the best illumination; and much else, although there was practically no chemistry involved. Lavoisier did not win the contest—indeed nobody did, for the prize was divided into smaller awards; but a gold medal, specially authorized by the king, was presented to him at the Easter public session of the Academy on 9 April 1766, a month after he had read to that body a second paper on gypsum.

Later that month Lavoisier's supporters in the Academy entered his name in the list of candidates for the place of *adjoint chimiste* that had fallen vacant. Needless to say, Lavoisier, at the age of twenty-two, was the youngest postulant. The winner, Louis Cadet de Gassicourt, like most of the others, was some ten years his senior. Nevertheless, Lavoisier's confidence was unabated; just prior to this election he drafted two similar letters, to be signed by one or more of his friends in the Academy; one was addressed to Mignot de Montigny (the president of the Academy for that year), the other to the perpetual secretary, Grandjean de Fouchy. Both letters urged the Academy to create a new division or class of *physique expérimentale*.[12] If Lavoisier hoped to make room for himself in this rigidly structured and exclusive body, nothing came of this early example of his ambition and overwhelming self-confidence; the letters probably were never sent. But that Lavoisier was serious about the importance of experimental physics we need hardly doubt; he thought of himself, then and later, as a *physicien*, an experimental physicist, even more than as a chemist. Only when his investigations dealt with the reactive or combinatorial behavior of substances (as in the paper on gypsum) did Lavoisier speak of doing chemistry. When, on the other hand, he investigated the physical "instruments" that bring about or influence chemical change—water, elastic fluids like air, imponderable fluids like heat or electricity—this was physics; he was wont, characteristically, to refer to Boyle and Priestley as *physiciens*, not as chemists. There is further proof of his sincerity; in 1785, when the Academy of Sciences underwent its last reorganization before the Revolution—and this was largely Lavoisier's achievement—a *classe de physique générale* was finally established.

Lavoisier was not easily discouraged. In 1767,

during his trip through the Vosges with Guettard, he received optimistic news from his father about his chances of election. Indeed, he seems to have taken his success for granted. On the title page of a copy of Agricola's *De re metallica*, which he purchased in Strasbourg in September, he wrote confidently: "Antonius Laurentius Lavoisier Regiae Scientiarum Academiae Socius anno 1767."[13]

In the spring of 1768 Lavoisier read to the Academy of Sciences a paper on hydrometry describing an accurate instrument of the constant-immersion type which he had designed. This was followed by the reading of a long paper on the analysis of samples of water he had collected in the course of his travels with Guettard. Then, as now, Europeans ascribed remarkable curative properties to the waters of various spas; and already there had grown up a large medico-chemical literature on mineral waters. Before Lavoisier, these were the only waters commonly analyzed. The method employed was first to identify by qualitative analysis the principal salt in a given sample; the concentration of this salt was then determined by evaporating a certain volume of water to dryness and weighing the solid residue. Lavoisier distrusted this method, for the salt could be lost by decrepitation, spattering, volatilization, or in some cases by decomposition. His method was to determine the concentration of the characteristic salt by making specific-gravity measurements of the water sample with his improved hydrometer, a method which was, of course, limited to waters containing a single salt. Typically, Lavoisier did not concern himself with the analysis of mineral waters—which, he wrote, were important·for only a small number of privileged persons—but with the potable waters used by society as a whole: waters from springs, wells, and rivers. He analyzed some samples in the field, but the best of his many measurements were made at the virtually constant temperature of the deep cellars of the Paris astronomical observatory.

Water, as we have seen, fascinated Lavoisier; he spoke of it as *l'agent favori de la nature* and as the chief agent in shaping the earth, producing all its crystal forms (including the diamond!). Analysis of waters ought to give some clue, he believed, to the kinds of hidden strata through which water flowed before emerging as a spring or river. The tables that accompanied this paper reveal his objective: the first table lists his analyses of water found in the inclined granitic and schistose strata of the Vosges, where all of his samples were more or less rich in Glauber's salt (hydrated sodium sulfate). The second table, analyzing water samples collected in the *bande calcaire,* disclosed a marked quantity of selenite or gypsum, with traces of sea salt.

Lavoisier's election to the Academy followed

shortly upon the reading of this paper. The Academy's vote was divided between Lavoisier and Gabriel Jars, a mining engineer for the royal government, with Lavoisier receiving a slight majority. When, according to established practice, the two top names were submitted to the king's minister, the Comte de St. Florentin, Jars was designated *adjoint chimiste* but a special dispensation was accorded Lavoisier, who was admitted, to the great joy of his father and his aunt, as *adjoint chimiste surnuméraire.*

Shortly before his election, in March 1768, Lavoisier entered the Ferme Générale, a private consortium that collected for the government such indirect imposts as the tax on tobacco and on salt (the *gabelle*), as well as customs duties and taxes on produce entering Paris. Having inherited a considerable fortune from his mother, he now invested a substantial portion of his capital by assuming a third of the interest of the farmer-general, François Baudon, in a lease *(bail)* negotiated under the name of a certain Jean d'Alaterre. Some of Lavoisier's future colleagues in the Academy of Sciences feared these responsibilities would detract from his scientific work. Others, like the astronomer Lalande, supported Lavoisier by arguing that his increased wealth made it unnecessary for him to seek other ways of earning a living. Indeed, so the story goes, one mathematician remarked, "Fine. The dinners he will give us will be that much better."

For the next few years, much of Lavoisier's time was taken up with journeys, as a traveling inspector (*tourneur*), on behalf of the Ferme Générale. One of these expeditions, from July to November 1769, took him across Champagne to inspect tobacco factories and check on the deployment of brigades assigned to catch smugglers. The early months of 1770 found him at Lille in Flanders; in August he was in Amiens, where he read a paper on the mineralogy of France (especially Picardy) at a public session of the Academy of Amiens. In the same year, again combining scientific work with his official travels, he presented a memoir on the water supply of Rouen to the academy of that city.

In 1771 Lavoisier married Marie–Anne–Pierrette Paulze, the only daughter of a farmer-general, Jacques Paulze. The discrepancy of age was notable: Lavoisier was twenty-eight, his bride not quite fourteen. Although the marriage was childless, it was happy and harmonious, a bourgeois marriage singularly devoid, it would seem, of anything other than fidelity and mutual esteem. Mme Lavoisier trained herself to be her husband's collaborator: she learned English (which he did not read), studied art with the painter David, and became a skilled draftsman and engraver. The thirteen copperplate illustrations in her husband's *Traité élémentaire de chimie* are her work; they are signed "Paulze Lavoisier sculpsit." In 1775, when Lavoisier was appointed a commissioner of the

Royal Gunpowder Administration (Régie des Poudres et Salpêtres), to serve in effect as scientific director, the couple took up residence in the Paris Arsenal.[14] Here Lavoisier equipped a fine laboratory where most of his later scientific work was carried out. Mme Lavoisier often assisted him, recording the results of experiments; and as his hostess to visiting scientific celebrities, and at weekly gatherings of his scientific colleagues, she proved an indefatigable promoter of the "new chemistry" and her husband's renown.

As Lavoisier himself insisted, concern for the public welfare was at least as important in directing his attention to the problem of water supply for Paris as was scientific curiosity. One of his earliest publications (in the *Mercure de France* for October 1769) was a reply to a certain Father Félicien de St. Norbert who had opposed a much-discussed plan to bring to Paris, by an open canal, the waters of the Yvette, a tributary of the Orge River. The plan had been proposed by an engineer, Antoine Deparcieux, who in memoirs read to the Academy of Sciences defended the feasibility of the project. The potability of the water of the Yvette and its purity seemed attested by experiments performed under the separate auspices of the Academy of Sciences and the Faculty of Medicine. Since these analyses involved weighing the solid residue obtained by evaporation to dryness, the question arose at the Academy whether it was true that water, on distillation, could be in part transmuted into earth; if so—and several early chemists believed this to be the case—then the method of evaporating to dryness was undependable. The transmutation problem was discussed by the physicist J.-B. Le Roy in a memoir presented at the Easter public meeting of the Academy in 1767. Le Roy did not believe that water could be changed into earth, but suggested instead that earth is somehow essential to the nature of water, or intimately associated with it, and that during distillation water and earth pass over together into the receiver. Nevertheless, the doctrine of transmutation had the authority of J. B. Van Helmont and of Robert Boyle, each of whom believed he had shown by experiment that the nutrition and growth of plants can only be attributed to water. Experiments like theirs were performed by various eighteenth-century scientists, chief among them the German physician Johann Theodor Eller, who found support for this doctrine by an experiment in which earth appeared to be formed when water was subjected to violent and prolonged shaking in a closed vessel and by experiments, performed with hyacinth bulbs, similar to the plant experiments of Van Helmont and Boyle.

4. The Problem
of the Elements

The question of the transmutation of water, which had puzzled so many, Lavoisier was to solve, not long after his election to the Academy of Sciences, by means of an experiment that was to make his name widely known and satisfy that craving for public recognition which was already a marked aspect of his character. He began in the late summer of 1768 with attempts to obtain distilled water of the highest purity for use as a standard in his hydrometric measurements. Pure rain water, he found, when repeatedly distilled, always left behind a small solid residue, yet with no appreciable change in its specific gravity. It occurred to him that the solid matter might have been produced during the distillation, perhaps from the glass, some of which might have been dissolved by the boiling water. To settle the question, he placed the sample of water, which he had repeatedly distilled, in a carefully cleaned and weighed glass vessel called a pelican, a vessel so designed that water-vapor condensed in a spherical cap, then descended to the bottom through two handle-like tubes, only to be vaporized once more. Before placing the apparatus on a sand-bath, he weighed the pelican with its contained water (obtaining thereby, by difference, the weight of water). He began the refluxing on 24 October 1768, continuing it for 101 days. After a few weeks he noted the appearance of particles of solid matter. When he stopped the experiment on 1 February 1769, he weighed the apparatus, finding no appreciable change in weight. Then transferring the water and the solid matter to another glass container, Lavoisier dried the pelican, reweighed it and found it significantly lighter. When he weighed the earthy particles, and evaporated the water to dryness, weighing the solid residue, he found the total amount of the solid matter roughly equal to the loss in weight of the pelican. Clearly, the earthy material (silica) had been dissolved from the glass and was not the result of a transmutation of the water.

This well-known experiment demonstrates Lavoisier's experimental ingenuity and those gravimetric procedures that were to characterize his later work. The research was written up and initialed *(paraphé)* by the secretary of the Academy early in 1769; yet the paper was not read until November 1770. Lavoisier's discovery, presented in a public session, was promptly noted by the press; but impatient to see the results in print and unwilling to await the leisurely publication of the *Histoire et mémoires* of the

Academy, Lavoisier profited from the establishment of a new scientific journal, the Abbé Rozier's *Observations sur la physique, sur l'histoire naturelle, et sur les arts*. A reference to Lavoisier's experiment appeared in a note in the first number of this journal (July 1771), and an extended summary was published in the second (August) number. Lavoisier's full account did not appear in the *Histoire et mémoires* until 1773.

This famous experiment may have had a practical aim, but its theoretical significance was probably foremost in Lavoisier's mind: water, he had shown, was not transmuted into earth and was probably an unchangeable element. We now know that as early as 1766 Lavoisier had begun to speculate about the nature of the traditional four elements, stimulated by two papers of J. T. Eller published in the *Memoirs* of the Berlin Academy. In these papers Eller rejected the doctrine of four elements and defended instead the notion that the true principles of nature were the "active" elements, fire and water. Water, as Eller believed he had shown by experiment, could produce earth. Lavoisier's experiment had pretty well disposed of this contention. But more interesting to Lavoisier was Eller's suggestion that air was the result of a combination of water with the matter of fire. This identification of water vapor with air can best be understood in the light of eighteenth-century theories about air and vapors. Air was the elastic body par excellence, playing its role (in combustion, for example) as a physical rather than a chemical agent. Vapors, on the other hand, were not thought to be inherently elastic but to be foreign particles dispersed and dissolved in air, just as particles of salt are dissolved in water. Nevertheless, scientists (Wallerius and Eller among them) had shown that water could evaporate in a vacuum, where there was no air into which the particles of water could be dissolved. Moreover, the increase in barometric pressure in the receiver of an air pump after the evaporation of water suggested to Eller that the water had been transformed into air by combining with the matter of fire.

In May 1766, Lavoisier jotted down two notes inspired by a rapid reading of Eller's papers; these papers struck him as "very well done." In the first of his notes he recorded Eller's notion that air might not be an element but a combination of water with the matter of fire. In his second note he developed his own theory, ignoring Eller's identification of water vapor with air. Instead, he suggested that air, by being combined with the matter of fire, might be a fluid in a permanent state of expansion. The elements, Lavoisier wrote, enter into the composition of all bodies; but this combination does not take place in the same manner in all bodies. There is a great similarity between the aerial fluid and the igneous fluid. Both lose a part of their (characteristic) properties when they combine with bodies. It is known, for example, that air when combined ceases to be elastic and occupies a space infinitely less than when it was free.

This last comment is a clear allusion to the work of Stephen Hales, who, in a long chapter of his *Vegetable Staticks,* had demonstrated that air could exist "fixed" in a wide variety of animal, vegetable and mineral substances. Hales's book had been translated in 1735 by Buffon, and Lavoisier doubtless first learned of Hales's experiments on "fixed air" from the lectures of Rouelle. But he may have been impelled by a reference in one of Eller's papers to turn directly to the *Vegetable Staticks.* In the years that followed, Lavoisier was to puzzle over this problem of the elements, with his attention focused increasingly upon the fixation of air and the possibility that the aeriform state resulted from the combination of some base with the matter of fire.

A key idea drawn from his reading of Hales was that the effervescence produced in various chemical reactions was not merely the result of the thermal agitation accompanying the reaction, or "fermentation," but was instead the sudden release of "fixed air." In 1768 Lavoisier called attention to a phenomenon (observed long before by the chemist E.-F. Geoffroy) that certain effervescent reactions produce a cooling effect.[15] This appeared to refute the belief that effervescences were simply the result of strong intestine motion of particles and that the heat, as some scientists believed, observed in other effervescent reactions was the result of friction. Moreover, it supported his notion that the air so released combined with the "matter of fire." Not long afterward, sometime between 1769 and 1770, Lavoisier became familiar with another phenomenon that supported his notion that air might be a combination of a base with the "matter of fire."

The observation of the Scots physician William Cullen (and of Lavoisier's compatriot Antoine Baumé) that when highly volatile liquids like ether or alcohol are vaporized, there occurs a pronounced drop in temperature, was strong support for this theory, for the simplest explanation was that the change from liquid to vapor was accompanied by the absorption of heat or the "matter of fire." In 1771—as yet unaware of Joseph Black's unpublished discoveries concerning latent heat—Lavoisier observed that when ice melts, although heat is steadily applied to it, the temperature of an ice-water mixture remains unchanged. Clearly, "fire" becomes "fixed," unable to affect the thermometer.

All these scattered bits of evidence were given clear meaning when Lavoisier encountered—just when, we are not certain—a remarkable article entitled "Expansibilité" in the *Encyclopédie* of Diderot and d'Alembert. The author of this anonymous article was the economist, philosopher, and public servant Turgot. Turgot defined "expansibilité," a word he seems to have coined, to mean unlimited elasticity, like that of air. But to Turgot not merely air, but all vapors, are expansible, a property they acquire when heat, or the subtle matter of fire, enters bodies and weakens the attractive forces binding the particles together. Common air is simply a particular vapor, or what Lavoisier would have called an aeriform fluid; if it were possible to lower the temperature sufficiently, it should be possible to liquefy it. And Turgot made the remarkable suggestion, later taken up by Lavoisier, that all substances are in principle capable of existing in any of the three states of matter—as solid, liquid, or aeriform fluid (gas)—depending upon the amount of the matter of fire combined with them. Sometime before the summer of 1772 Lavoisier had drafted an incomplete but remarkable memoir which he called "Système sur les éléments" and which outlined a covering theory—if we may call it that—which was henceforth to guide his own investigations and his interpretation of the findings of others. The elements, notably water, air, and fire, can exist in either of two forms, fixed or free. In the crystals of certain salts, water is fixed as "water of crystallization." Air is not only fixed in many substances but even enters into the composition of mineral substances. The same is true

74

of "phlogiston or the matter of fire." But how, he asks, can air, a fluid capable of such remarkable expansion, be fixed in solid substances and occupy such a small space? The answer is his *théorie singulière*, according to which water exists in the atmosphere as a vapor in which the particles are combined with the fine, elastic particles of the matter of fire; and the air we breathe is not a simple substance but a special kind of fluid combined with the matter of fire.

Up to this point, these were only private speculations which Lavoisier set down in several unpublished drafts. He had performed no experiments, and the theory derived entirely from his reading and the inferences he drew from the discoveries of others. But in the course of 1772 some new facts came to Lavoisier's attention and led to his famous first experiments on combustion, the dramatic first steps toward his "revolution in chemistry."

5. The Chemical Revolution —First Phase

The revolution in chemistry has been summed up as the overthrow of the phlogiston theory (the new chemistry was later called the antiphlogistic chemistry), but this is only part of the story. His eventual recognition that the atmosphere is composed of different gases that take part in chemical reactions was followed by his demonstration that a particular kind of air, oxygen gas, is the agent active in combustion and calcination. Once the role of oxygen was understood—it had been prepared before Lavoisier, first by Scheele in Sweden and then independently by Priestley in England—the composition of many substances, notably the oxyacids, could be precisely determined by Lavoisier and his disciples. But the discovery of the role of oxygen was not sufficient of itself to justify abandoning the phlogiston theory of combustion. To explain this process, Lavoisier had to account for the production of heat and light when substances burn. It is here that Lavoisier's theory of the gaseous state, and what for a time was his theory of the elements, came to play a central part.

At this point, we may ask what Lavoisier could have known about the work of the British pneumatic chemists other than Stephen Hales. The answer would seem to be "very little." Of Joseph Black, often described as a major influence upon him, Lavoisier clearly knew nothing at first hand until 1773 or perhaps late 1772, for Black's famous *Essay on Magnesia Alba* was for long unavailable in French. Yet Black's major achievements were summarized in the French translation (1766) of David MacBride's *Experimental Essays on Medical and Philosophical Subjects*, a work strongly indebted to Hales and Black, and chiefly concerned with the possible medical uses of Black's "fixed air" (carbon dioxide). Although Lavoisier had the book in his library, there is no evidence that he was impressed by it. On the other hand Jean Bucquet, a physician and chemist whom Lavoisier admired, and who later became his collaborator, had his interest in the chemistry of air aroused by MacBride's book. In his *Introduction à l'étude des corps naturels tirés du règne minéral* (2 vols., Paris, 1771), Bucquet remarks that air is found in almost all bodies in nature, in almost all minerals, although perhaps not in metals. He discusses the rival views of J. F. Meyer and MacBride on the causticity of alkalis and quicklime, and describes the precipitation of calcareous matter when "fixed air" is passed through limewater.

77

The famous paper of Henry Cavendish on "fixed air" long remained unknown, and it was some time before Joseph Priestley's work could serve as a stimulus to inquiries about different kinds of air. In March 1772, Priestley reported to the Royal Society the experiments that later appeared in the first volume of his *Observations on Different Kinds of Air*, a work only published late in 1772. Some faint echoes of his discoveries did reach the French chemists during the spring; what especially attracted their attention was Priestley's discovery that vitiated air is restored by the gaseous exchange of plants, and his report that an English physician had cured putrid fever by the rectal administration of "fixed air." It was not, however, these vague reports that made Frenchmen aware of Priestley's activity, but rather his first publication on gases, a modest pamphlet entitled *Directions for Impregnating Water with Fixed Air*, which appeared in June 1772 and was soon translated into French. Here again it was the presumed medical use of such artificial soda water that accounts for the impression it made. Yet we can only conclude that in 1772 the book by Stephen Hales was the predominant influence in interesting Lavoisier in the chemical role of air.

Early in 1772, at all events before June of that year, there appeared a book by the provincial lawyer and chemist Louis–Bernard Guyton de Morveau, which conclusively proved that the well-known gain in weight of lead and tin when they are calcined is not a peculiarity of those metals, but that all calcinable metals become heavier when transformed into a calx; moreover, this increase has a definite upper limit characteristic of each metal. Guyton sought to explain these results by invoking a fanciful variation of the phlogistic hypothesis, but Lavoisier suspected that the fixation of air might be the cause. By August he had devised an experiment to determine the role that air might play in chemical reactions involving metals. Was air absorbed by or released from a metal when exposed to the strong heat of a burning glass? Perhaps it would be possible to answer this question by using an apparatus devised by Stephen Hales (his pedestal apparatus) which enabled the amount of air released or absorbed to be measured. Soon after, however, Lavoisier learned that a Paris pharmacist, Pierre Mitouard, had reported that when phosphorus was burned to form the acid, air seemed to be absorbed.

In the early autumn of 1772 Lavoisier carefully verified this report. He burned weighed quantities of phosphorus and sulfur and discovered that the acids produced weighed more than the starting materials and absorbed, notably in the case of sulfur, "a prodigious amount of air." Soon after, using a modification of Hales's pedestal apparatus, he heated minium (red lead) in the presence of charcoal in a closed vessel and observed that a large amount of air was given off. This discovery struck him as "one of the most interesting of those that have been made since the time of Stahl."[16] Accordingly, he followed the common practice of the Academy of Sciences to assure priority and recorded these results in a famous sealed note *(pli cacheté)* deposited with the secretary of the Academy.

These experiments confirmed Lavoisier's suspicions that air, or some constituent of air, played an important role in the processes of combustion and calcination. In the autumn of 1772 he set himself to read everything that had been published on aeriform fluids. Translations were soon made available (probably through the indefatigable transmitter of scientific gossip Jean–Hyacinthe Magellan) not only to Lavoisier but also to such of his fellow chemists in France as Bucquet, Hilaire-Marin Rouelle (the brother of Lavoisier's teacher), and the pharmacist Pierre Bayen, all of whom investigated, late in 1772 and in early 1773, the production and properties of Black's "fixed air."[17]

On 20 February 1773, Lavoisier opened a new research notebook (the first of his famous *registres de laboratoire*) with a memorandum announcing his intention to embark on a "long series of experiments" on the elastic fluid emitted from bodies during various chemical reactions and on the air absorbed during combustion. The subject was obviously so important—

"destined," as he put it, "to bring about a revolution in physics and chemistry"—that he proposed in the succeeding months to repeat all the early experiments and to extend his own.

His experiments during the winter and early spring of 1773 dealt largely with the calcination and reduction of metals. On 20 April, at the Easter public session of the Academy of Sciences, Lavoisier for the first time made his results public, in "A New Theory of the Calcination and Reduction of Metallic Substances." This theory or its elaboration, he generously conceded, owed much to conversations with his friend Trudaine de Montigny. It is easily summarized: metallic calces are formed when metals combine with a certain quantity of "fixed air"; reduction of these calces consists in the release of this same air; and it is this air, abundant in the atmosphere, which causes the increase in weight that metals acquire during calcination.

It is evident from this paper, which he never published, and from his laboratory records, that Lavoisier was undecided whether to attribute these effects to atmospheric air, to some unknown portion of the atmosphere, or to Black's "fixed air." Yet that some sort of air was taken up and evolved in these processes, as well as in the experiments with phosphorus and sulfur, was clearly evident. On 5 May, at a regular meeting of the Academy, the famous

81

sealed note of the previous November was opened and its contents read. In the succeeding months, Lavoisier appeared at successive meetings of the Academy, reporting on his experiments and outlining what he had learned of the history of "fixed air." In September certain of the key experiments were repeated in the presence of a specially appointed Academy committee which included P.-J. Macquer and J.-C.-P. Trudaine de Montigny. The results of all this activity formed the substance of Lavoisier's first book, the *Opuscules physiques et chimiques,* which was published in January 1774.

6. Oxygen and Its Role

In 1774 two French chemists, Pierre Bayen and Cadet de Gassicourt, investigated the peculiar behavior of red calx of mercury *(mercurius calcinatus per se)*. From this substance, they claimed, the metal could be regenerated without the addition of a reducing agent rich in phlogiston, like charcoal, simply by heating it to a higher temperature. Was this true? And was this "red precipitate of mercury," as Lavoisier called it, a true calx?[18] Early in the autumn of 1774 the subject was discussed at the Academy of Sciences, and Lavoisier was made a member of a committee to examine this question. But before the inquiry could be made, there occurred an episode about which much ink has been spilt.

In October the English chemist Joseph Priestley, during a visit to Paris, dined with Lavoisier and a group of other French scientists. Priestley told the assembled guests that in the previous summer he had obtained a new kind of air by heating the "red precipitate of mercury." The air was poorly soluble in water, and in it a candle burned more brightly than in common air. Priestley had, in fact, prepared oxygen; but at the moment he thought he had found a species of nitrous air (nitric oxide), a gas he had discovered earlier.

Since Lavoisier, not long after, turned to investigate this new air, Priestley may be pardoned for believing that Lavoisier was simply following his clue. Many scholars have accepted Priestley's claim, but it is certainly not true.[19] Lavoisier and the other members of the Academy committee were already familiar with the "red precipitate of mercury" and reported in November that it was reduced without addition. If this substance was a true calx, Lavoisier did not need Priestley's disclosure to know that an air would be released when it was reduced. Indeed, Pierre Bayen, one of the first to call attention to the strange behavior of the red precipitate, had actually found that a gas was given off on reduction, although he erred in claiming that it was Joseph Black's "fixed air."

Lavoisier took up this question seriously in the early months of 1775. He collected the air produced by the reduction of mercury calx and tested it, not to see if it had the properties of Priestley's new air, which did not immediately occur to him, but to determine whether or not it was "fixed air," first by passing the gas through limewater (which it did not precipitate), then by seeing whether it would extinguish a flame. He recorded in his notebook that "far from being extinguished," the flame burned more brightly than in air.[20] He concluded that the air was "not only common air ... but even more pure than the air in which we live."

At the public session of the Academy on 26 April 1775, Lavoisier described his discoveries in a paper entitled "Mémoire sur la nature du principe qui se combine avec les métaux pendant leur calcination, et qui en augmente le poids." Determined as usual to bring out his results as soon as possible and aware that the *Histoire et mémoires* of the Academy was several years behind schedule, Lavoisier published this classic paper (in its first version) in the May issue of Rozier's *Observations sur la physique*.

Meanwhile, Priestley was not idle. With a new sample of the red precipitate purchased in Paris, he again took up the investigation soon after his return to England. Various tests, carried out early in 1775, convinced him that he had not prepared nitrous air but had discovered a new gas "between four and five times as good as common air." A firm advocate of the phlogiston theory, he assumed—because this gas supported combustion so much better than common air—that it must be a better receptacle for phlogiston, had less phlogiston already in it, and should be called "dephlogisticated air." Priestley published these experiments and his conclusion in the second volume of his *Experiments and Observations on Different Kinds of Air*, which appeared before the end of 1775.

If Lavoisier owed little or nothing to Priestley's earlier disclosure, his indebtedness to Priestley at this point in time is undeniable. Advance sheets of Priestley's volume reached Paris by December,[21] and Lavoisier saw at once the significance of the new facts they contained. He set to work to confirm and extend Priestley's work; preparing once more the air from the mercury calx, he referred to it in his laboratory notebook as "the dephlogisticated air of M. Prisley [sic]."[22] He noted that calcining mercury would be a way of analyzing atmospheric air into its chief components. In April 1776 he studied the residual air left after prolonged calcination of mercury, which of course was mainly nitrogen; and although he found that like Black's "fixed air" it did not support combustion, yet it did not precipitate limewater. He followed this analysis, according to his custom, by a synthesis: he mixed five parts of the residual air with one part of "dephlogisticated air" and found that a candle burned in it about as brightly as in common air. The highly respirable property of "dephlogisticated air" soon commanded his attention.

When in 1778 Lavoisier reread to the Academy of Sciences his classic paper of three years earlier and published it in the Academy's *Mémoires*, he revised it without making it clear that he had changed his conclusions—and, indeed, recast the paper—because of what he had learned from Priestley's book and from his own subsequent experiments. Priestley, to be sure, is not mentioned. But Lavoisier no longer described the air produced by reducing mercury calx (without addition) as highly pure atmospheric air; now he called it "the purest part of the air" or "eminently respirable air." This air, he also showed, combines with carbon to produce Black's "fixed air," which he was soon to call, since it was known to be weakly acidic and to combine with alkalis and alkaline earths to form what we call the carbonates, "chalky aeriform acid" *(acide crayeux aériforme)*.

Lavoisier's activity during these years was prodigious; his scientific productivity was at its peak, and the experiments that he performed alone or with his collaborator, Jean Bucquet, contributed to round out his theory. Several main lines of inquiry were pursued simultaneously: the properties of aeriform fluids, the mystery of vaporization and heat, the role of "eminently respirable air" in combustion and respiration, and the formation of acids. This last was to add a new dimension to his oxygen theory.

7. Theory of Acids

Considerable progress had been made during the eighteenth century toward understanding the behavior of acids.[23] Rouelle, Lavoisier's teacher, had confirmed that salts were combinations of an acid with certain substances that served as a "base" (alkalis, earths, and metals); and he had shown that certain salts were genuinely neutral while others contained an excess of acid. New acids, too, were identified; beginning with his preparation of tartaric acid in 1770, the great Swedish chemist Carl Wilhelm Scheele added nearly a dozen organic acids to the roster of new chemical individuals, as well as preparing acids from such metals as arsenic and tungsten.

As to the cause of acidity, various theories were current—for example, Newton's doctrine that acids were substances "endued with a great attractive force, in which their activity consists," a theory favored by Macquer and Guyton de Morveau. Lavoisier, on the other hand, thought in more traditional terms and believed it possible to identify the "constituent principles" of acids and bases, just as his predecessors had analyzed salts into their two major constituents. One widely held notion was that there was one fundamental or "universal" acid, of which the individual acids were simply modifications. Various acids were nominated for this distinction, including vitriolic (sulfuric) acid and Black's "fixed air," which Bergman called the "aerial acid."

The sharp, fiery taste of acids led to a confusion of acidity with the causticity of such substances as corrosive sublimate or quicklime. Joseph Black had argued that the causticity of quicklime was an inhering property that was masked when the lime combined with "fixed air." A chemist and apothecary of Osnabrück, J. F. Meyer (1705–1765), attacked Black's theory and argued that mild alkalis become caustic when they take up an oily acid, *acidum pingue*, as he believed limestone does when it is burned to quicklime. The calxes of metals, Meyer thought, might contain *acidum pingue*. This imaginary protean substance, closely related to fire and light, was also the "universal primitive acid" of which all other acids were modifications.

As early as 1766, Lavoisier was familiar with Meyer's theory, for in his notes on Eller's memoirs he makes a passing reference to *acidum pingue*. When he wrote the *Opuscules* in 1773, Lavoisier had not definitely decided in favor of Black's theory rather than Meyer's; both theories of causticity were presented on their merits, although Lavoisier wrote of Meyer's book that it contained a "multitude of experiments, most of them well made and true," and noted that the theory of *acidum pingue* explains "in the most natural and simple fashion" the gain in weight of metals on calcination. Should Meyer's ideas be adopted, the result would be nothing less than a new theory directly contrary to that of Stahl.[24]

It is likely that Lavoisier at first shared the widespread notion that a universal acid, whether or not it was an *acidum pingue*, was to be found in the atmosphere and that this primitive acid gave rise to all the particular acids known to the chemist. His important step forward was to abandon the notion, essentially tautological, that an acid gave rise to acids and to suggest that an identifiable chemical substance, in fact an aeriform fluid or gas, played this universal role of acid-former. Yet before the autumn of 1772 Lavoisier did not suspect that air entered into the composition of acids. When air was released in the reaction between an acid and a metal, as in the production of "inflammable air" (hydrogen), Lavoisier believed that it came from the metal. In his August Memorandum of 1772 he wrote that "air enters into the composition of most minerals, even of metals, and in great abundance." Yet his experiments with phosphorus and sulfur convinced him that when they were burned to form the acids, air was absorbed. In the *Opuscules* of 1774 Lavoisier could remark that phosphoric acid was "in part composed of air, or at least of an elastic substance contained in air."

He did not return to the subject until two years later. On 20 April 1776, Lavoisier read to the Academy one of his most brilliant papers, a memoir entitled "Sur l'existence de l'air dans l'acide nitreux." Referring back to his experiments on phosphorus and sulfur, and his conclusion that air entered into the composition of the acids resulting from the combustion of these substances, he was led to consider the nature of acids in general and to conclude that all acids were in great part made up of air; that this substance was common to all of them; and, further, that they were differentiated by the addition of "principles" characteristic of each acid. When he "applied experiment to theory," Lavoisier was able to confirm his suspicion that it was the "purest portion of the air," Priestley's dephlogisticated air, that entered without exception into the composition of acids, and especially of nitric acid, which was particularly deserving of study because of the importance of saltpeter (potassium nitrate) in the making of gunpowder.

The experiments were as follows. When a known quantity of nitric acid was heated with a weighed amount of mercury, the resulting product was a white mercurial salt (mercuric nitrate); this decomposed to form the red oxide, yielding *air nitreux* (nitric oxide). On further heating, the red oxide, as Lavoisier already knew, decomposed, producing metallic mercury and the "air better than common air," or "eminently respirable air." Lavoisier was careful to separate the different gaseous fractions by collecting the air under different bell jars over water. According to his practice, the analysis was followed by a synthesis: by bringing together the nitric oxide and the "pure air" in the presence of a small amount of water, he was able to regenerate nitric acid.

Almost exactly a year later, on 21 March 1777, Lavoisier read a memoir to the Academy of Sciences in which he showed that phosphorus burned in air combines with the "eminently respirable air" to form phosphoric acid. When this air is used up, the remaining air, which he called *mofette atmosphérique* (nitrogen), does not support combustion or sustain life. In the same paper he showed that sulfur takes up "eminently respirable air" in the formation of vitriolic acid.

In 1779 Lavoisier brought together the results of all this work in an important paper (published in 1781) entitled "Considérations générales sur la nature des acides." Here are set forth his conclusions that since "eminently respirable air" is a constituent of so many acids, it may play the role of "universal acid" or, rather, of the "acidifiable principle." When combined with carbonaceous substances or charcoal, this air forms chalky acid (carbon dioxide); with sulfur, vitriolic acid; with nitric oxide, nitric acid; with phosphorus, phosphoric acid. When combined with metals, on the other hand, it forms calxes (oxides). Nevertheless, it was the acid-forming characteristic that impressed him; he therefore proposed to call the acidifying principle or base of "eminently respirable air" the "oxygen principle" *(principe oxigine)*, that is, the "begetter of acids." What he soon called "vital air"[25] he described, faithful to his conception of aeriform fluids, as a combination of the "matter of fire" with a base, the "principe oxigine." By 1787, when the collaborative *Nomenclature chimique* was published, *oxigine* had become *oxygène*. In the meantime he had extended the application of his oxygen theory of acids and had discovered that there existed related acids that differed only in the proportion of oxygen they contained, as for example sulfurous and sulfuric acids; the higher the degree of oxygenation, he discovered, the stronger was the acid produced. In a paper published in 1785 Lavoisier made an equally important contribution by proving that the solution of metals in acids was a form of calcination: a calcination by the "wet way" *(par la voie humide)*. The metal combines with a quantity of the *principe oxigine* approximately equal to that which it is capable of removing from the air in the course of ordinary calcination.

Scholars have generally pointed to Lavoisier's theory of acids as perhaps his major error, or at least as a rash induction. From his analysis of a number of the oxyacids (carbonic, sulfuric, nitric) and certain organic acids (oxalic and acetic), all shown to contain oxygen, he argued that all acids must be so constituted, although he readily admitted that muriatic (hydrochloric) acid had not been shown to contain oxygen, which indeed it does not. Lavoisier explained this away by assuming that so far it had resisted further analysis.

8. The Constitution of Water

Other gases besides oxygen interested Lavoisier (the term "gas" was soon to replace the word "air" or the phrase "aeriform fluid"),[26] and none more than the "inflammable air" produced by the action of weak acids on iron or copper. In September 1777 with Bucquet he burned this "inflammable air" to see whether, as Bucquet expected, "fixed air" was produced, as was the case in the combustion of carbon. The limewater test was negative. What, then, was the product formed?

After the death of Bucquet, Lavoisier repeated this experiment in the winter of 1781–1782, using what he called a gasholder or pneumatic chest (*caisse pneumatique*) to store the oxygen and maintain a steady flow into a bottle filled with "inflammable air." Persuaded that some acid should be formed when the two gases were burned together, he was surprised when once more he failed to detect any product or even a trace of acidity. Convinced that something must have been produced, since the basic article of scientific faith, on which his quantitative procedures were based, was that matter is neither created nor destroyed in chemical reactions, Lavoisier determined to carry out the

95

experiment "with more precision and on a larger scale." To this end, assisted by his younger colleague, the mathematician Laplace, he designed a combustion apparatus in which streams of the two gases, each stored in a pneumatic chest, could be brought together in a double nozzle and burned together.

Before this new apparatus was completed, Lavoisier used the first pneumatic chest in a spectacular experiment in which a stream of oxygen, directed into a hollowed-out piece of charcoal, burned at such a high temperature that it melted platinum, a recently described metal that had resisted fusion even at the temperature of the great burning glass of Trudaine. Lavoisier reported his success at the public session of the Academy of Sciences on 10 April 1782. Early in June, and at considerable expense, he transported his equipment to the Academy and demonstrated, in the presence of a visiting Russian grand duke (traveling incognito as the Comte du Nord), the melting of a small mass of platinum by what Benjamin Franklin, another observer, called a fire "much more powerful than that of the strongest burning mirror," indeed the "strongest fire we yet know."[27]

Lavoisier's combustion apparatus was ready by June 1783 and was immediately put to historic use. In that month the Academy of Sciences was visited by the assistant of Henry Cavendish, Charles Blagden, a physician and scientist who the following year was to

THE CONSTITUTION OF WATER

become the secretary of the Royal Society. Blagden, so the familiar account runs, informed Lavoisier and some other members of the Academy of Sciences that Cavendish had obtained pure water when he had detonated a mixture of "inflammable air" and "dephlogisticated air" in a closed vessel. As Blagden recalled this event, the French scientists replied that they had already heard about such experiments as repeated by Joseph Priestley but doubted that the weight of water, as Cavendish claimed, was equal to the weight of the gases used. They believed, rather, that the water was already contained in, or united to, the gases used. Nevertheless, Blagden's disclosure supported what they had already learned. Accordingly, Lavoisier and Laplace put into action the newly completed combustion apparatus. On 24 June 1783, in the presence of Blagden and several academicians, they burned substantial amounts of the dry gases and obtained enough of the liquid product so that it could be tested. It did not give an acid reaction with litmus or syrup of violets, precipitate limewater, or give a positive test with any of the known reagents; it appeared to be "as pure as distilled water." In reporting on these experiments, Lavoisier confessed that it was not possible to be certain of the exact quantity of the gases that were burned; but, he argued, since in physics, as in mathematics, the whole is equal to the sum of its parts, and since only water and nothing else was formed, it seemed safe to conclude that the weight of the water was the sum of the weights of the two gases from which it was produced.

With the return of the Academy in November from its vacation, Lavoisier read at the public meeting an account of his experiments, making the historic announcement that water was not a simple substance, an element, but a compound of the *principe oxigine* with what he proposed to call the "aqueous inflammable principle" *(principe inflammable aqueux)*, that is, hydrogen. A summary of these results appeared anonymously in the December issue of Rozier's journal.[28] A draft of this summary in Lavoisier's hand, recently identified in the archives of the Academy of Sciences, proves beyond a doubt that he was the author.[29] The fuller and more elaborate memoir, published after Lavoisier had begun extensive work with J.-B.-M. Meusnier, appeared in the Academy's *Mémoires* in 1784.[30]

9. The First Balloon Ascensions

The summer and autumn of 1783 riveted public attention, and that of the scientific community (including that shrewd American observer, Benjamin Franklin), upon the dramatic success of the first lighter-than-air flights. Soon after the pioneer demonstrations by the Montgolfier brothers came the historic exploit of the Marquis d'Arlandes and Pilatre de Rozier, who made the earliest manned free ascent. The hot air "aerostats," as the balloons were called, could be made to rise or descend only by varying the intensity of the fire of straw or other light combustible which caused hot air to rise into the open bottom of the balloon.

A quite different, and far more promising, solution was soon proposed and demonstrated by J.-A.-C. Charles, a free-lance teacher of physics. With his assistants, the brothers Robert, he launched an unmanned balloon that had been laboriously filled with "inflammable air." On 1 December, Charles and the younger Robert took off from the Tuileries in a basket *(nacelle)* lifted by a hydrogen-filled balloon twenty-six feet in diameter; they rose to the height of 300 fathoms: driven by a southeast wind, they covered a distance of nine leagues before an uneventful descent. Then Charles went aloft alone, rose to the height of nearly 1,700 fathoms, showing physicists, Lavoisier wrote, "how one can rise up to the clouds to study the causes of meteors."[31] What particularly impressed Lavoisier was the complete control Charles and Robert had over their machine, using bags of sand to regulate the ascent of the balloon and descending by venting hydrogen.

Meanwhile, the Academy of Sciences appointed a standing committee to find measures for improving balloons, by determining the best shape, ways of maneuvering them, and above all by finding "a light gas, easy to obtain and always available, and which would be cheap" with which to fill the balloons. The committee included, besides the Academy's officers, physicists like J.-B. Le Roy, Mathurin Brisson, and Coulomb, and chemists like Berthollet and Lavoisier, who—as he habitually did when serving on committees—became its secretary. Attached to this group was J.-B.-M. Meusnier, a young officer on leave from the Corps of Engineers. A graduate of the military engineering school at Mézières, he had been since 1776 a corresponding associate *(correspondant)* of the Academy of Sciences. The ease with which "inflammable air" had been obtained from the decomposition

100

of water convinced Lavoisier that this was the route to follow in obtaining in quantity the cheap, light gas sought by the committee. In this inquiry, carried out in his laboratory at the Arsenal, Lavoisier had the invaluable assistance of Meusnier. In March 1784 they produced a small amount of the inflammable air by plunging a red-hot iron into water; later that month they successfully decomposed water by passing it drop by drop through an incandescent gun barrel. In this fashion Meusnier and Lavoisier prepared eighty-two pints of the light, inflammable air, and on 29 March they repeated this experiment in the presence of members of the standing committee. Meusnier presented the results of this joint effort to the Academy on 21 April; the full memoir was published soon after.

Steps were now taken to carry out with high precision a really large-scale decomposition of water into its constituent gases and its synthesis. Meusnier radically redesigned Lavoisier's gasholders *(caisses pneumatiques)* to allow the volume of gas and the rate of outflow to be measured with accuracy. These earliest "gasometers," as well as a combustion flask for the large-scale synthesis of water, were the work of the instrument maker Pierre Mégnié.

The experiments were carried out at the Arsenal on 27 and 28 February 1785, in the presence of members of a special evaluation committee of the Academy and other invited guests. For the decomposition

101

experiment, water was percolated through a gun barrel filled with iron rings; the inflammable air was collected in bell jars over water in a pneumatic trough, from which it was transferred to a gasometer. In one experiment the amount of the gas (expressed in weight equivalents of water) was found to be equal to well over 335 *livres* of water. These experiments, in the opinion of Daumas and Duveen, exceeded all previous chemical investigations in "the perfection of the equipment used, the scale upon which the work was carried out, and the importance of the conclusions to be derived from the results."[32] On 19 March, Berthollet, who had followed these experiments closely, wrote to Blagden of the recent keen interest "in the beautiful discovery of Mr. Cavendish on the composition of water," remarking that "Mr. Lavoisier has tried to bring to this matter all the accuracy of which it is capable."[33] Water, all but a few intransigent opponents were now obliged to admit, was not the ir- reducible "element" it had always been thought to be but a compound of the oxygen principle with the inflammable air that was soon to be baptized "hydro- gen," the begetter of water.

10. The Study of Heat

The demonstration of the compound nature of water put the capstone on Lavoisier's oxygen theory of combustion. For a number of years Lavoisier had been reluctant to come out openly in opposition to the phlogiston theory, nor had he been in a hurry to publish his speculations about the nature of "aeriform fluids" or gases.[34] Not enough evidence was at hand to support his theory that gas was only a state which substances acquire when they are combined with a sufficient amount of the "matter of fire." His studies of heat were inspired by a desire to support what came to be called his "caloric" theory.

In the spring of 1777 Lavoisier had enlisted the cooperation of his young colleague at the Academy, Laplace, in experiments on the vaporization of water, ether, and alcohol in the evacuated receiver of an air pump.[35] These experiments convinced Lavoisier that under proper conditions of temperature and pressure, these fluids could be converted into vapors which, like air, existed "in a state of permanent elasticity." Emboldened by these results, Lavoisier presented in November 1777 the substance of one of his most famous papers, "Mémoire sur la combustion en général," the earliest announcement of his theory of combustion and his first, albeit cautious, assault on the phlogiston theory.

When Lavoisier resumed his collaboration with Laplace in 1781, the two soon undertook (1782–1783) a famous series of experiments, using a piece of apparatus—the ice calorimeter—and a technique, both suggested by Laplace.[36] With this contrivance the heat given off by hot bodies when they cooled, by exothermic chemical reactions, or by animals placed within the apparatus, was measured by the amount of water produced by the melting of ice. With their calorimeter Lavoisier and Laplace determined the specific heats of various substances, the heats of formation of different compounds, and measured the heat produced by a guinea pig confined for several hours in their apparatus. Laplace read an account of these experiments to the Academy on 18 June 1783; their classic joint "Mémoire sur la chaleur" was published as a pamphlet later that summer and, essentially unaltered, in the *Histoire et mémoires* of the Academy in 1784. For Lavoisier, certain of these experiments on heat were convincing proof of his theory of vaporization, which held that gases owe their aeriform, elastic state to their combination with a large amount of the "matter of fire"; and so the heat and light given off during combustion must come from the fire–matter released from the "vital air" (oxygen gas) when the oxygen principle combines with a combustible substance.

It has been argued that Lavoisier's caloric theory merely transferred the phlogiston from the combustible to the "vital air," and there is something to this view. Like phlogiston, the fire-matter was a weightless fluid (or at least too tenuous to be weighed); nevertheless, unlike phlogiston, which defied measurement, both the intensity (the temperature) and the extensive measure of the fire (the heat produced in a given period of time) could be precisely measured. These calorimetric experiments, together with the work on water, seemed to Lavoisier to complete the evidence for his theory of combustion; and in 1786 he published his definitive attack on the old theory, "Réflexions sur le phlogistique." A brilliant dialectical performance, rightly called "one of the most notable documents in the history of chemistry,"[37] it is a closely reasoned refutation not only of Stahl but also of those latter-day phlogistonists, such as Macquer and Antoine Baumé, who had tried to modify Stahl's hypothesis in the light of the new experimental evidence.

The "Réflexions" was a personal manifesto, but it did not serve to convince all French scientists. Some, like Baumé, like Joseph Priestley, remained recalcitrant to the end. But the most tireless antagonist was the physician and naturalist Jean-Claude de La-métherie. Lavoisier's exact contemporary (he was born in September 1743), he was a prolific author of generally wordy, often slovenly works on natural history, natural philosophy, geology, and chemistry. Never admitted to the Academy of Sciences, he yet occupied an influential position, for in 1785 he became editor of Rozier's old journal, the *Observations sur la physique*. La métherie, a devoted and uncritical disciple of Priestley, was violently opposed to Lavoisier's theories; the *Observations*, therefore, which had once been so hospitable to Lavoisier, became—to a degree—the journal of the opposition.

11. The Campaign for the New Chemistry

During the years 1785–1789 a number of able chemists came over to Lavoisier's camp: Claude Berthollet, who had been converted when he closely followed the work on the decomposition and synthesis of water; Antoine de Fourcroy, the student of Lavoisier's former collaborator Bucquet; and Guyton de Morveau. These men, forming with Lavoisier and his wife what we might call the "antiphlogistic task force," set out to convert the scientific world to the "new chemistry." The instruments they employed were several and well selected—intended to attract the young and the uncommitted.

First of all, to persuade a new generation of chemists to join their ranks and to complete what Lavoisier had envisaged since 1773—a revolution in chemistry—the task force brought out a collaborative work, the *Méthode de nomenclature chimique* (1787). Originally suggested by Guyton de Morveau to eliminate the confused synonymy of chemistry, and prefaced by a memoir of Lavoisier, it emerged as a complete break with the past. In effect the scheme was based upon the new discoveries and theories, a fact that led the aging Joseph Black to complain that to accept the new nomenclature was to accept the new French theories. In a series of tables the *Nomenclature* listed the elements *(substances non décomposées)*, that is, those bodies that had not been, or perhaps could not be, decomposed. Fifty-five in number, these simple bodies included light and Lavoisier's "matter of fire," now called "caloric"; the elementary gases: oxygen, *azote* (nitrogen), and "inflammable air," now called hydrogen; carbon, sulfur, and phosphorus; the sixteen known metals; a long list of organic "radicals" (i.e. acidifiable bases); and the as yet undecomposed alkaline earths and alkalis. Compounds were designated, as chemists have done ever since, so as to indicate their constituents: the metallic calxes were now called oxides; the salts were given names indicating the acid from which they are formed (sulfates, nitrates, carbonates, and so on). The *Nomenclature*—translated into English, German, Italian, and Spanish—was extremely influential and widely read.

A second expression of the collective effort was a French translation of Richard Kirwan's 1784 *Essay on Phlogiston.* This translation, made by Mme Lavoisier, was published in 1788, the year after the *Nomenclature chimique*, and was copiously annotated with critical notes by members of the task force: the chemists Guyton de Morveau, Berthollet, and Fourcroy; the physicists and mathematicians Monge and Laplace; and, of course, Lavoisier himself.

A third and most important instrument was the establishment of a new scientific journal, edited—and dominated—by the votaries of the "new chemistry." The first number of this journal, the *Annales de chimie*, appeared in 1789, the year of the Revolution. Its editors were, besides Lavoisier, his early disciples— Guyton, Berthollet, Fourcroy, and Monge—with the addition of three new recruits: the Strasbourg metallurgist the Baron de Dietrich, Jean-Henri Hassenfratz, and Pierre-Auguste Adet.

Constituting still another, and much underestimated, vehicle for diffusing the new ideas were the later editions of Fourcroy's *Élémens d'histoire naturelle et de chimie*.[38] Of this immensely popular work a third edition, completely recast in terms of the "new chemistry," was published toward the end of 1788. A fourth edition appeared in 1791 and a fifth in 1793; it was translated into English, Italian, German, and Spanish. Its influence cannot be exaggerated, for it was one of the richest compendia of up-to-date chemical fact before the appearance of Thomas Thomson's *System of Chemistry* (1802). It was, moreover, the first work to present the whole of chemistry, as then known, in the light of Lavoisier's doctrines and according to the new nomenclature.

109

ANTOINE-LAURENT LAVOISIER

The last—and the best-known—of the propaganda instruments was Lavoisier's classic book, his *Traité élémentaire de chimie* (1789). The culmination of Lavoisier's achievement, it grew out of the *Nomenclature*—indeed, it was a sort of justification of it. Neither a general reference work nor a technical monograph, this small work was a succinct exposition of Lavoisier's discoveries (and those of his disciples) and an introduction to the new way of approaching chemistry. Significantly, it begins, after the famous "Discours préliminaire," with an exposition of that theory of vaporization and the states of matter which had guided Lavoisier throughout much of his scientific career.

On 2 February 1790, Lavoisier sent his venerable friend Benjamin Franklin two copies of his *Traité élémentaire de chimie,* one for Franklin himself, the other for the American Philosophical Society, of which he was a foreign member. In a letter to Franklin, he commented on his book, his approach to chemistry, and his pedagogical purpose:

In all the treatises on chemistry published since Stahl, the writers have always begun by setting forth a hypothesis and then have striven to show that with this assumption all the phenomena of chemistry could be tolerably well explained.

I believe, and a large number of scientists today agree with me, that the hypothesis accepted by Stahl

110

and subsequently modified is false, that phlogiston in the sense that Stahl gave to this word does not exist, and it was chiefly to develop my ideas on this subject that I undertook the treatise that I have the honor to send you.

I tried, as you will see in the preface, to reach the truth through the close linking up [*enchaînement*] of facts, to dispense with speculation as much as I could, for it is a treacherous instrument which deceives us, in order to follow as much as possible the torch of observation and experiment.

This course, which had not yet been followed in chemistry, led me to plan my book according to an absolutely new scheme, and chemistry has been brought much closer than heretofore to experimental physics. I very much hope that your leisure and your health will allow you to read the first chapters of it, since your approval, and that of a few European scientists who are without prejudice in these sorts of matters, is all that I desire.

It seems to me that chemistry presented in this way has become infinitely easier to learn than it was before. Young people whose heads are not filled with any system grasp it eagerly, whereas older chemists still reject it, and most of them find it more difficult to grasp and to understand than those who have not yet studied any chemistry.

French scientists are at present divided between the old doctrine and the new. I have on my side M. de Morveau, M. Berthollet, M. de Fourcroy,

M. de La Place, M. Monge, and in general the physicists of the Academy. The scientists of London and of England also very gradually abandon Stahl's doctrine, but the German chemists still cling to it. So here we have a revolution that has taken place in an important area of human knowledge since your departure from Europe. I shall hold this revolution to be well advanced and even completed if you will line up with us.

As Lavoisier made clear to Franklin, the preface, or "Discours préliminaire," a defense of the new chemistry with its new nomenclature, is also a short essay on scientific pedagogy, and on the proper method of scientific inquiry. The most widely read of Lavoisier's writings, it opens with quotations from the *Logique* (1780) of the Abbé de Condillac: language is the instrument of analysis; we cannot think without using words; the art of reasoning depends upon a well-made language *(l'art de raisonner se réduit à une langue bien faite)*. The *Traité*, Lavoisier remarks in this prefatory essay, grew out of his work on the nomenclature which, "without my being able to prevent it," developed into an elements of chemistry. This must be taken with a grain of salt, for in notes set down in 1780–1781 Lavoisier had already outlined an elementary treatise, to be prefaced with two preliminary *discours*, one of which closely resembles the "Discours préliminaire" of 1789 and was intended to treat the application of logic to the physical sciences, especially chemistry. The notes for this preface, with page reference to the *Logique* in the margin, cite the same passages from Condillac that Lavoisier eventually used in print.

The epistemological and psychological assumptions Lavoisier outlines in the "Discours préliminaire" of 1789 are the commonplaces of eighteenth-century thought, found not only in Condillac, but in d'Alembert and in Rousseau's *Emile*: at birth, the mind is a *tabula rasa*; all our ideas come from the senses; analysis—that shibboleth of the Enlightenment—is the only way to truth; even a small child analyzes his experience; nature, through deprivation and pain, corrects his errors in judgment.

The beginning student of physical science must follow the path nature uses in forming the ideas of a child. His mind must be cleared of false suppositions, and his ideas should derive directly from experience or observation. But a scientific Emile is not promptly corrected by nature through the pleasure-pain principle; men are not punished for the hypotheses they invent, which their amour-propre leads them to elaborate and cling to. Because the imagination and reason must be held in check, we must create an artificial nature through the use of experiment.

Lavoisier gives numerous examples of the speculative notions that often hamper the progress of chem-

113

istry. He derides the order commonly followed in works on chemistry, which begin by treating the elements of bodies *(principes des corps)* and explaining tables of affinity. This latter branch of chemistry he acknowledges to be important (perhaps the best calculated to make chemistry eventually a true science), but it is not fully warranted by experiment, and is unsuited to an elementary treatise. As to the elements, all we can say about their nature and number amounts to mere metaphysical talk. And if by elements we mean those simple, indivisible particles *(molécules)* that bodies are made of, it is likely that we know nothing about them. Even the existence of his cherished caloric fluid, although it explains the phenomena of nature in a very satisfactory manner, is a mere hypothesis.

The chief operation of chemistry is to determine by analysis and synthesis the composition of the various substances found in nature; chemistry advances toward its goal by dividing, subdividing, and subdividing still again. If we mean by the elements of bodies the limit reached by this subdivision, then all the substances we are unable to decompose are to us as the elements out of which the other substances are made. In the *Traité* these substances are called *substances simples*; yet Lavoisier confesses: "We cannot be certain that what we regard today as simple is really so; all that we can say is that such a substance is the actual limit reached by chemical analysis, and that, in the present state of our knowledge, it cannot be further subdivided."

When we compare the table of *substances simples* in the *Traité* with that given in the *Nomenclature* two years earlier, we note some interesting changes. First, the list has been drastically reduced and now contains only thirty-three substances. Nineteen organic radicals and the three alkalis (potash, soda, and ammonia) have been eliminated, and with some justification. There was increasing evidence that the organic radicals could be broken down—in the *Traité* Lavoisier himself reports the composition of the "acetic radical"—and the case of the alkalis was similar. In 1785 Berthollet had shown that ammonia consists only of hydrogen and nitrogen, and presumably Lavoisier believed that potash and soda would also turn out to be compounds of familiar substances.

Both in the *Nomenclature* and the *Traité* the tables of undecomposed or simple substances are divided into subgroups, five in the first case, four (with the elimination of the alkalis) in the second. But in both tables the first subgroup is distinguished from the rest. In the *Nomenclature* this is made up of light, caloric, oxygen, and hydrogen. In the *Traité*, nitrogen *(azote)* has been added, and here for the first time these substances are described surprisingly as "simple substances which belong to the three kingdoms and

115

which one can consider as the elements of bodies." It is curious that these five substances appear to Lavoisier to have more claim to the status of elements than other simple bodies, for example sulfur, phosphorus, carbon, or the metals.

The principal justification is revealed in a note Lavoisier set down in 1792 where he writes: "It is not enough for a substance to be simple, indivisible, or at least undecomposed for us to call it an element. It is also necessary for it to be abundantly distributed in nature and to enter as an essential and constituent principle in the composition of a great number of bodies." Wide distribution, and its presence in a great number of compounds, qualifies a substance to be called an element. Gold, on the other hand, is a simple substance, yet it is not an element. But there is something more to Lavoisier's conception of an element: he specifically notes that such a substance "enters as an essential and constituent principle" in compound bodies. In the older chemistry, from which Lavoisier is unable to free himself completely, the elements—the four elements of Aristotle, the *tria prima* of Paracelsus, and so on—were thought of as the bearers and the causes of the distinctive qualities of bodies into which they enter. As we saw in discussing his theory of acids, Lavoisier had strong ties to this "chemistry of principles." So in his first subgroup the substances deserving to be called elements act in this special way. Thus caloric is the "principle" that accounts for a body's physical state. Oxygen, of course, conveys acidity. Hydrogen is the producer of water, that essential substance found in all the realms of nature. But what of light and of nitrogen? Lavoisier never quite satisfied himself about the nature of light, but he knew from the work of Ingen-Housz and Senebier that light plays an essential part in the gaseous chemistry of vegetation, a matter to which he alluded in a remarkable speculative paper he published in 1788. Nitrogen, to be sure, is everywhere in the earth's atmosphere and is widely distributed in animal and vegetable substances. But was this sufficient reason for Lavoisier to elevate it to the dignity of an "element" of the first subgroup? Quite possibly he gave it this higher status because he tended to think, on the basis of Berthollet's analysis of ammonia, that nitrogen might be the "principle" of all alkalis, what Fourcroy would have liked to call "alkaligène."

Lavoisier's *Traité*, albeit an elementary textbook, contains important material much of which he had not previously published, notably his pioneer experiments on the combustion analysis of organic compounds and on the phenomenon of alcoholic fermentation, which impressed him as "one of the most striking and the most extraordinary" effects observed by the chemist. He was aware that the combustion of substances of vegetable origin, such as sugar and alcohol, yielded water and carbon dioxide; but he was convinced that these compounds did not exist preformed in the substances burned—which, however, do contain the elements hydrogen, oxygen, and carbon. Lavoisier's first combustion analyses involved burning various oils in a rather complicated apparatus shown in one of the plates of the *Traité*. A simpler contrivance was devised for the combustion of highly volatile substances like alcohol and ether. In his analysis of alcohol he determined the ratio of hydrogen to carbon by weight to be 3.6 to 1, not far from the correct value of 4 to 1.

Like his immediate predecessors—Macquer, for example—Lavoisier distinguished three kinds of fermentation: vinous or spirituous fermentation, acid or acetous fermentation (such as produces acetic acid), and putrid fermentation. He did not speculate about the underlying cause of these processes, although he took for granted the existence of some sort of "ferment," but confined himself to the chemical changes. Vinous or alcoholic fermentation, marked by a violent intestine motion, he saw to be a chemical reaction involving rearrangement of the three essential organic "principles": oxygen, hydrogen, and carbon. He assumed an equality or "equation"[39] between the amount of these elements in the original sugar and the amount in the end products: alcohol, carbon

118

dioxide, and acetic acid. His experiments seemed to bear out his assumption. His data, however, were wholly unreliable, although the end result was correct. As Arthur Harden put it: "The research must be regarded as one of those remarkable instances in which the genius of the investigator triumphs over experimental deficiencies." The numbers reveal grave errors, and "it was only by a fortunate compensation of these that a result as near the truth was attained."[40]

In describing his work on fermentation in chapter XIII of the *Traité*, Lavoisier stated most clearly his principle of the conservation of matter in chemical reactions:

> Nothing is created either in the operations of the laboratory, or in those of nature, and one can affirm as an axiom that, in every operation, there is an equal quantity of matter before and after the operation; that the quality and quantity of the principles are the same, and that there are only alterations and modifications. On this axiom is founded the whole art of making experiments in chemistry: we must suppose in all of them a true equality or equation between the principles of the body one examines, and those that we extract [*retire*] by analysis.[41]

12. Physiological Research

Despite his prolonged interest in the chemistry of respiration, which had preoccupied him on and off since his earliest work on combustion, Lavoisier deliberately omitted all references to the subject in his *Traité élémentaire de chimie*. When in his earliest experiments on different kinds of air Lavoisier exposed small animals to these gases, it was less to explore the phenomenon of respiration than to characterize the gases. He was already aware that "fixed air" asphyxiated animals and that atmospheric air, "corrupted and infected" by the respiration of man or animals, takes on the character of "fixed air." In his *Opuscules physiques et chimiques*, where he summarized Priestley's experiments and recounted his own, Lavoisier advanced a physical, rather than a chemical, explanation of respiration. The role of atmospheric air, he then believed, is to inflate the lungs; "fixed air" is unable to do this because, being highly soluble in water, it is taken up by the moisture of the lungs "and suddenly loses its elasticity." In an atmosphere of "fixed air," therefore, the action of the lung is suspended and the animal suffocates.[42]

It was only after his first experiments with "dephlogisticated air" (oxygen) and his discovery that, far from killing animals, this gas "seemed, on the contrary, better fitted to sustain their respiration"[43] than ordinary air, that Lavoisier turned to the problem of respiration: it had now become a problem of physiological chemistry. His earliest experiments were carried out at the Château de Montigny near Paris with Trudaine de Montigny during the Academy's vacation (October 1776).[44] He read the results at the Easter public session on 9 April 1777, under the title "Mémoire sur les changements que le sang éprouve dans les poumons et sur le mécanisme de la respiration."[45] By this time he could assert that respiration involved only the *air éminemment respirable* (oxygen), and that the remainder of the air is purely passive, entering and leaving the lung unchanged. In the course of respiration animals take in the *air éminemment respirable*, which is either converted into *acide crayeux aériforme* (carbon dioxide) or is exchanged in the lung, the oxygen being absorbed and an approximately equal volume of carbon dioxide being supplied by the lung. Lavoisier tended to favor the first alternative. Indeed, in that same year, in his "Mémoire sur la combustion en général," he suggests in a concluding paragraph that this reaction is similar to the combustion of carbon and must be accompanied by the release of a certain amount of the matter of fire. This, he points out, may account for the

121

production of animal heat.[46] A persuasive argument seemed to him to be that, just as the calcination of mercury and lead results in red powders, so the absorption of oxygen gives a bright red color to arterial blood.

The calorimeter provided a new instrument for the quantitative study of animal heat and the verification of Lavoisier's combustion theory of respiration. In a famous experiment with Laplace they measured the heat produced by a guinea pig exhaling a given amount of carbon dioxide, comparing this figure with the heat of formation of the same amount of carbon dioxide produced by burning carbon in an atmosphere of oxygen. But the results showed a significant discrepancy: more heat was produced by the guinea pig than by the burning of carbon. It was soon discovered that the experimental animals gave off less carbon dioxide than the intake of oxygen had led them to expect. In a paper read before the Royal Society of Medicine in February 1785, Lavoisier argued that either some of the oxygen unites with the blood or it combines with hydrogen to form water.[47] Although not fully convinced, Lavoisier favored the second alternative; and in his last experiments, carried out in cooperation with Armand Seguin, he assumed that both carbon dioxide and water were produced. The collaborative work was begun in 1789 and reported to the Academy late in 1790 and in 1791. These experiments were more genuinely physiological than Lavoisier's early ones. Lavoisier and Seguin found that the quantity of oxygen consumed increases with the temperature and is greater during digestion and exercise. The combustion, according to their findings, occurs in the lung, more specifically in its tubules, into which the blood secretes a "humor" composed of carbon and hydrogen. Understandably, the pressure of events during the Revolution left Lavoisier little time for scientific work; experiments begun collaboratively were in some cases left for Seguin to complete. The most vivid records of these last experiments are the drawings made by Mme Lavoisier showing Seguin, his face covered by a mask, breathing air or oxygen to determine the amount consumed when at rest or at work.

13. Lavoisier and the French Revolution

The range of Lavoisier's activity is hard for lesser talents and less rigidly disciplined personalities to comprehend. To carry on his multifarious public responsibilities without neglecting his beloved science required a rigid and inflexible schedule. Mme Lavoisier tells us that he rose at six in the morning, worked at his science until eight and again in the evening from seven until ten. The rest of the day was devoted to the business of the Ferme Générale, the Gunpowder Administration, and meetings of the Academy of Sciences and of its numerous special committees. One day a week, his *jour de bonheur*, he devoted entirely to scientific experiments.[48]

Lavoisier rose steadily in the hierarchy of the Academy of Sciences. In August 1772 he was promoted to the rank of associate *(associé chimiste)*; he reached the top rank of *pensionnaire* in 1778. He served on a number of those committees set up at the request of the royal government to investigate matters of public concern. Among the most notable of these committees were those formed to investigate the condition of the prisons and hospitals of Paris and one, on which Lavoisier served with Benjamin Franklin, charged with investigating Mesmer's cures by what he called "animal magnetism."

Nor were his responsibilities confined to his official duties. Lavoisier's father, shortly before his death, purchased one of those honorific offices that carried with it the privilege of hereditary nobility. The title devolved on Lavoisier in 1775, and not long afterward he purchased the country estate of Fréchines, near Blois. Here he carried on agricultural experiments, chiefly concerned with the improvement of livestock, which he reported to the Royal Agricultural Society of Paris (to which he had been elected in 1783) and to the government's Committee on Agriculture, established soon after by Calonne, the minister of finance *(contrôleur général)*.

In sympathy with much of the criticism leveled against the *Ancien Régime*, Lavoisier shared many of the ideas of the *philosophes* and was closely associated with Pierre-Samuel Dupont de Nemours and other physiocrats. Politically liberal, and almost certainly a Freemason, he took an active part in the events leading to the Revolution. In 1787 he was chosen a representative of the third estate at the provincial assembly of the Orléanais, the province in which he was a landowner. He served on the important standing committee *(bureau)* that dealt with social conditions and agriculture; he wrote reports on the *corvée*, on charitable foundations, and on trade; and he was responsible for many far-reaching proposals: schemes for old-age insurance, charity workshops to give employment to the poor, and tax reform.

When, after a lapse of nearly two centuries, the famous Estates-General was brought into being once again to deal with France's mounting problems, Lavoisier was chosen as alternate deputy for the nobility of Blois; as secretary, he drafted their bill *(cahier)* of grievances, a remarkably liberal document that embodied many of his earlier proposals. Although he never served in the National Assembly, multiple activities occupied him during the years of the Revolution. He was elected to the Commune of Paris and took his turn with the National Guard. He joined the most moderate of the revolutionary clubs, the short-lived Society of 1789. For this self-appointed planning group, whose members included Condorcet, the economist Pierre-Samuel Dupont de Nemours, and the famous Abbé Siéyès, Lavoisier prepared his important paper on the *assignats*, pointing to the problems inherent in issuing paper money. Because of his mastery of financial matters, he was made a director of the Discount Bank (Caisse d'Escompte), established in 1776 by his patron Turgot; became an administrator of the national treasury; and in 1791 published a long report on the state of French finances. In the same year he brought out a classic statistical study of the agricultural resources of the country.[49] For the recently created Advisory Bureau for the Arts and Trades (Bureau de Consultation des Arts et Métiers) he helped draft, along with others, an elaborate scheme for the reform of the national educational system of France, based largely, to be sure, on ideas already put forward by Condorcet.

Lavoisier's letter to Franklin of 2 February 1790, cited earlier for its discussion of the revolution in chemistry, concludes—with a symmetry that can hardly have been accidental—by giving his views toward the great political revolution, and in words which show that Lavoisier was neither a radical nor a reactionary:

After having held forth to you about what is happening in chemistry, I should say something about our political revolution. We look upon it as achieved irreversibly. Nevertheless there still exists an aristocratic party which makes futile efforts and which is evidently very weak; the democratic party has on its side the greatest number and in addition education, philosophy and enlightenment. The moderates, who have kept their heads in this general turmoil, think that circumstances have carried us too far, that it is unfortunate to have been obliged to arm the common people and all the citizens; that it is ill advised to place force in the hands of those who should obey; and that it is to be feared that the establishment of the new constitution will be opposed by the very persons for whose benefit it has been made. . . .

We deeply regret at this time that you are so far from France; you would have been our guide, and you would have marked out for us the bounds that we should not have exceeded.[50]

Increasingly unhappy at the leftward thrust of the Revolution, Lavoisier still remained loyal to his country. In these critical years he was active in the Academy of Sciences (he served as its treasurer from 1791 until the abolition of that body), and took an important part in the most enduring of its accomplishments: the establishment of the metric system of weights and measures.[51] Until his arrest he was engaged, in collaboration with the crystallographer René-Just Haüy, in establishing the metric unit of mass (the gram). Together they measured with high precision the weight of a given volume of distilled water at different temperatures.

Despite his eminence and his services to science and to France, Lavoisier was the target of increasingly violent attacks by radical journalists like Jean-Paul Marat. One after another the institutions with which Lavoisier had been associated changed form or were abolished. He was removed from his post in the Gunpowder Administration in 1791 but remained at the Arsenal until 1793, when he severed all connections with the *Régie*. That year brought the Reign of Terror, the abolition of the Discount Bank and the suppression of all the royal learned societies, including the Academy of Sciences.

In 1792, at the height of his career, Lavoisier determined to bring together the many scattered papers in which he and his collaborators had laid the foundation of a new chemistry. For such troubled times, it was an ambitious project. Never a cloistered scientist, but a public-spirited reformer, he was faced with new responsibilities, especially his share in the great project of establishing the metric system, which left little time for research or writing. Yet he began in odd moments to assemble, and largely to rework, his earlier memoirs and articles, the fruit of thirty years of accomplishment.

The time was ill-chosen, for political events were moving with ominous rapidity toward the kind of régime which Lavoisier, a moderate constitutionalist, could not approve. In September of that year the monarchy was abolished, and in January 1793 Louis XVI led the long parade to the guillotine. In the ensuing Reign of Terror, men of Lavoisier's moderate views were treated as enemies of the Republic, driven from the Legislative Assembly, forced to flee for their lives. The attacks on Lavoisier grew in intensity, partly because of his conservative fiscal opinions, but above all for his association with the unpopular Gen-

129

eral Farm. His apartment was searched, and suspicious letters, mostly from his scientific friends in England, were impounded. Earlier, the National Assembly had abolished the Farm and set up a committee of experts (which did not include Lavoisier) charged with liquidating its affairs. This committee made slow progress and was accused of delaying tactics. On 24 December 1793 an order went out for the arrest of all the farmers-general. Lavoisier and his father-in-law, Jacques Paulze, were imprisoned with the others. After four months he was brought to trial before the Revolutionary Tribunal on the morning of 8 May 1794. Convicted with the others, he was publicly executed that afternoon on a guillotine erected on the Place de la Révolution; his body was trundled off to a nameless grave. The story that Lavoisier appealed at his trial for time to complete some scientific work and that the presiding judge replied, "The Republic has no need of scientists," is apocryphal.[52] Authentic, however, is the remark of Lagrange, shortly after Lavoisier's execution: "It took them only an instant to cut off that head, and a hundred years may not produce another like it." [53]

During the enforced leisure of his imprisonment, Lavoisier had corrected the proof sheets of the projected *Mémoires*. Part of a first volume, all of a second, and a small part of a fourth had been set up in type. The proofs, hastily and imperfectly corrected, were seized with the rest of Lavoisier's private papers. Eventually, in calmer times, they were returned to his widow. Anxious to pay tribute to her husband's memory and to support his claim to be the sole author of the new chemical theory, this gifted and devoted woman determined to publish the existing fragments. Unable to find a collaborator who would include in his introduction an indictment of those scientists who had failed to come to Lavoisier's aid at the time of his arrest, she undertook the work herself and had the book printed from the proof sheets, adding a brief and eloquent preface.

Cheaply and poorly printed, with missing pages at the end of each of the parts, checkered over with misprints, the undated two volumes of the *Mémoires de Chimie* appeared about 1803. The work was never put on public sale; instead, Mme Lavoisier presented copies to a few libraries and to a number of eminent scientists. Although no masterpiece of the printer's art, to historians of science these two volumes have great value. The heavily corrected, often rewritten, classic papers contain Lavoisier's final interpretation of his own discoveries and evidence of the continued vitality of this great mind cut off in full maturity. Perhaps he had just set aside these unfinished proofs when he wrote, in his last surviving letter from prison: "I have had a fairly long life, above all a very happy one, and I think I shall be remembered with some regrets and perhaps leave some reputation behind me. What more could I ask?" [54]

131

NOTES

BIBLIOGRAPHY

ILLUSTRATION CREDITS

INDEX

Notes

1. For Lavoisier's genealogy, see Edouard Grimaux, *Lavoisier*, 2nd ed., p. 326.
2. Now the rue Pecquay. See Jacques Hillairet, *Dictionnaire historique des rues de Paris*, 3d ed. (Paris, 1966), II, 250. The Turgot plan of Paris (1739) shows the cul-de-sac "Pequet" opening from the rue des Blancs-Manteaux, not far from the Palais Soubise (the present Archives Nationales). By Piganiol de la Force it was called "Cul-de-sac Pequai ou de Novion dans la rue des Blancs-Manteaux," in *Description de Paris* (Paris, 1742), 427.
3. Grimaux erroneously called it the rue du Four Saint-Eustache; its name was simply rue du Four, or rue du Four-Saint Honoré, although to distinguish it from the rue du Four on the Left Bank, letters to residents were sometimes addressed "rue du Four St. Honoré près St. Eustache." It is now the rue de Vauvilliers, running from the rue Saint Honoré to the rue Coquillière.
4. Not published in Lavoisier's lifetime, the piece on the aurora is printed in *Oeuvres de Lavoisier*, IV, 1–7.
5. Lavoisier papers, archives of the Academy of Sciences, dossier 424. Cited by Rhoda Rappaport in "Lavoisier's Geologic Activities," in *Isis*, **58** (1968), 377.
6. *Oeuvres de Lavoisier—Correspondance*, fasc. I, 1–3.
7. Guettard, "Mémoire qui renferme des observations minéralogiques," cited by Rappaport, *loc. cit.*, p. 376.
8. Guettard, "Mémoire sur la manière d'étudier la minéralogie," cited by Rappaport, ibid.
9. For a general appraisal of Rouelle and his course in chemistry, see Rhoda Rappaport, "G.-F. Rouelle: An Eighteenth-Century Chemist and Teacher," in *Chymia*, **6** (1960), 68–101.
10. *Oeuvres de Lavoisier*, III, 112.

11. The full title of this publication is *Mémoires de mathématique et de physique, présentés à l'Académie royale des sciences, par divers savans et lûs dans ses assemblées.*
12. These unsigned letters, which have puzzled scholars, are printed in *Oeuvres de Lavoisier—Correspondance*, fasc. I, 7–10, repr. from *Oeuvres de Lavoisier*, IV, 561–563.
13. The Agricola title page, with Lavoisier's inscription, is reproduced as pl. I of Denis I. Duveen, *Bibliotheca alchemica et chemica* (London, 1949). The book itself is now in the Lavoisier Collection at Cornell University.
14. For the early history of the powder industry in France, see Régis Payan, *L'évolution d'un monopole: L'industrie des poudres avant la loi du 13 fructidor an V* (Paris, 1934). The *régie* was established by Turgot to replace the earlier *ferme*. See Douglas Dakin, *Turgot* (London, 1939), 164–166; and Edgar Faure, *La disgrâce de Turgot* (Paris, 1961), 108–110.
15. In a paper entitled "De la manière de composer des feux d'artifices colorés en bleu et en jaune," deposited as a sealed note on 14 May 1768. See *Oeuvres de Lavoisier—Correspondance*, fasc. I, 107–108. A significant reference by Lavoisier to the ideas of Hales about the fixation of air appeared in a paper of the same year. See J. B. Gough, "Lavoisier's Early Career in Science," in *British Journal for the History of Science*, **4** (1968), 52–57. More detailed early references to Hales's experiments are given in Lavoisier's "Sur la nature de l'eau," published in 1773, and in his *Opuscules physiques et chimiques* of 1774.
16. This famous phrase appears in Lavoisier's *pli cacheté* of 1 Nov. 1772. Repro. in Henry Guerlac, *Lavoisier—The Crucial Year* (Ithaca, N.Y., 1961), 227–228. In "The Origin of Lavoisier's First Experiments on Combustion," *Isis,* **63** (1972), 349–355, Robert E. Kohler, Jr., argues that the experiments on phosphorus and sulfur were performed to explore the composition of acids and were not stimulated by a primary interest in the combustion and calcination of metals as I first argued in my article "The Origin of Lavoisier's Work on Combustion," *Archives*

Internationales d'Histoire des Sciences, **12** (1959), 114–135. Kohler's paper is worth serious consideration, but besides the fact that Lavoisier's August Memorandum of 1772 discusses the possible role of air in minerals and metals, there is the further fact that Lavoisier's first public disclosure of his work (the paper read on 21 April 1773 and first published by René Fric) dealt preponderantly with the calcination and reduction of metals, mentioning the sulfur and phosphorus experiments almost as an afterthought.

17. The first of these translations, a *précis raisonné* of a memoir by a follower of Joseph Black, N. J. von Jacquin, was published in Rozier's *Observations sur la physique* in February 1773. Translations of Joseph Black's classic paper on magnesia alba, Joseph Priestley's "Observations on Different Kinds of Air," and Daniel Rutherford's paper on mephitic air (nitrogen) appeared in the spring and early summer in the same journal.

18. On this question, see a paper by C. E. Perrin, "Prelude to Lavoisier's Theory of Calcination—Some Observations on *mercurius calcinatus per se,*" in *Ambix,* **16** (1969), 140–151.

19. In September 1774 the Swedish chemist Scheele communicated to Lavoisier a method of making oxygen by heating a preparation of silver carbonate. This letter was not published in *Oeuvres de Lavoisier—Correspondance,* fasc. II. See Uno Boklund, "A Lost Letter From Scheele to Lavoisier," in *Lychnos* (1957), 39–62. Boklund virtually accused the French scholars, including René Fric, of suppressing the letter so as to give all credit to Lavoisier, although he was aware that Grimaux had published this letter long before, as "Une lettre inédite de Scheele à Lavoisier," in *Revue générale des sciences pures et appliquées,* **1** (1890), 1–2. In any case Lavoisier seems to have been too preoccupied with other matters to follow up Scheele's suggestion.

20. M. Berthelot, *La révolution chimique,* 264–265.

21. See letters of Magellan (or Magalhaens) to Lavoisier in *Oeuvres de Lavoisier—Correspondance,* fasc. II, 504–508.

22. Berthelot, *op. cit.*, p. 271.

23. Much of this section is dependent upon Maurice Crosland's article "Lavoisier's Theory of Acidity," *Isis,* **64** (1973), 306–325.

24. *Oeuvres de Lavoisier,* I, 482.

25. In a paper published in the *Histoire et mémoires* of the Academy in 1784, Lavoisier adopted, at the suggestion of Condorcet, the term *air vital* for what he had previously called (after Priestley) "dephlogisticated air" or "eminently respirable air." *Oeuvres de Lavoisier*, II, 263.

26. Originally a term used by Van Helmont to signify "a Spirit that will not coagulate," it was applied particularly to noxious vapors like firedamp. In the 1st ed. (1766) of his *Dictionnaire de chimie*, P. J. Macquer applied the term to "the volatile invisible parts which escape from certain bodies," for example, "the noxious vapors which rise from burning charcoal, and from matters undergoing spirituous fermentations." But in the 2nd ed. (1778) of the *Dictionnaire* he applied the word generally to aeriform fluids. See, for example, the articles "Gas ou air déphlogistiqué" and "Gas méphytique ou air fixe." In the same year Jean Bucquet included in his *Mémoire sur la manière dont les animaux sont affectés par différens Fluides Aériformes* an introductory section entitled "Histoire abrégé des différens Fluides aériformes ou Gas." The spelling used by both men is "gas," not "gaz." It is possible that this generalized use of the term "gas" may have been influenced by the second edition (1777) of James Keir's trans. of the first ed. of Macquer's *Dictionnaire* to which Keir appends *A Treatise on the Various Kinds of Permanently Elastic Fluids, or Gases.* A MS French translation of this treatise survives among Lavoisier's papers.

27. *Writings of Benjamin Franklin*, Albert Henry Smyth, ed., VIII (1906), 314.

28. *Observations sur la physique*, **23** (1783), 452–455. The paper is entitled "Extrait d'un mémoire lu par M. Lavoisier, à la séance publique de l'Académie royale des sciences, du

12 novembre, sur la nature de l'eau."
29. By C. E. Perrin. See his "Lavoisier, Monge and the Synthesis of Water," *British Journal for the History of Science,* **6** (1973), 424–428.
30. *Oeuvres de Lavoisier,* II, 334–359. Lavoisier notes that certain additions were made relative to the work done with Meusnier.
31. *Ibid.,* III, 733. See Benjamin Franklin's letters to Sir Joseph Banks, *Writings of Benjamin Franklin,* IX (1906), 79–85, 105–107, 113–117, and 119–121. On 16 September 1783 Franklin wrote to Richard Price: "All the Conversation here at present turns upon the Balloons fill'd with light inflammable Air, and the means of managing them, so to give men the Advantage of Flying." *Ibid.,* pp. 99–100.
32. Maurice Daumas and Denis I. Duveen, "Lavoisier's Relatively Unknown Large-Scale Decomposition and Synthesis of Water," in *Chymia,* **5** (1959), 126–127.
33. *Ibid.,* 127.
34. Two anonymous attacks on the phlogiston theory published in Rozier's *Observations sur la physique* in 1773 and 1774 have been widely attributed to Lavoisier—for example, by Berthelot, McKie, and Duveen. For arguments against Lavoisier's authorship and suggestions of likely alternatives, see Carleton Perrin, "Early Opposition to the Phlogiston Theory: Two Anonymous Attacks," in *British Journal for the History of Science,* **5** (1970), 128–144.
35. Henry Guerlac, "Laplace's Collaboration With Lavoisier," in *Actes du XIIᵉ Congrès international d'histoire des sciences, Paris, 1968,* III B (Paris, 1971), 31–36.
36. Mme Lavoisier's drawing of the ice calorimeter is given in pl. VI of Lavoisier's *Traité élémentaire de chimie.* Two versions have survived and are in the collection of the Conservatoire des Arts et Métiers in Paris. It has not been possible to determine with certainty which of Lavoisier's artisans built the calorimeters, but it was probably a tinsmith named Naudin. See Maurice Daumas, *Lavoisier théoricien et expérimentateur* (1955), p. 142 and notes, and the illus-

trations in his "Les appareils d'expérimentation de Lavoisier," in *Chymia*, **3** (1950), 45–62, fig. 3.

37. Douglas McKie, *Antoine Lavoisier* (London–Philadelphia, 1935), p. 220.

38. For Fourcroy, and his relations with Lavoisier, see W. A. Smeaton, *Fourcroy, Chemist and Revolutionary, 1755–1809* (Cambridge, 1962).

39. J. R. Partington calls this the first use of the word "equation" in our modern sense of "chemical equation." Lavoisier's example is: must of grapes = carbonic acid + alcohol. See Partington's *History of Chemistry*, III, 480.

40. Arthur Harden, *Alcoholic Fermentation* (London, 1911), p. 3. Partington has remarked (*History of Chemistry*, III, p. 376) that Lavoisier "aimed at accurate results, but seldom achieved them." Guichard (*Essai historique sur les mesures en chimie* [Paris, 1937], 54–60), after examining Lavoisier's numerical results, judged his precision extremely variable; indeed in the later, more complicated experiments the accuracy was less than in the earliest ones. Yet Lavoisier repeatedly stressed the importance of quantitative accuracy. In the *Traité* he writes: "La détermination du poids des matières et des produits, avant et après les expériences, étant la base de tout ce qu'on peut faire d'utile et d'exact en chimie, on ne saurait y apporter trop d'exactitude" (*Oeuvres de Lavoisier*, I, 251); elsewhere he writes "Rien n'est supposé dans ces explications, tout est prouvé, le poids et la mesure à la main" (*ibid.*, V, 270).

41. *Oeuvres de Lavoisier*, I, 101. The axiom that matter is neither created nor destroyed originated with the atomists of antiquity. It was clearly stated by Mariotte in his *Essai de logique* (1678) and was a common assumption of eighteenth-century scientists. But Lavoisier deserves credit for applying it specifically to the operations of the chemist and for spelling out a law of the conservation of matter in chemical reactions.

42. *Ibid.*, 520–521, 625–627.

43. "Mémoire sur la nature du principe qui se combine avec

les métaux pendant leur calcination, et qui en augmente le poids," in *Observations sur la physique,* **5** (1775), 433.
44. Berthelot, *op. cit.,* 290–291.
45. Cited from the *Procès-verbaux* of the Academy of Sciences by Maurice Daumas, in *Lavoisier, théoricien et expérimentateur,* p. 38. Daumas says this remained unpublished, yet it was almost certainly published, with the inevitable modifications, in 1780 as "Expériences sur la respiration des animaux." See *Oeuvres de Lavoisier,* II, 174–183.
46. *Ibid.,* 232.
47. "Altérations qu'éprouve l'air respiré," *ibid.,* 676–687.
48. Charles C. Gillispie, "Notice biographique de Lavoisier par Madame Lavoisier," in *Revue d'histoire des sciences et de leurs applications,* **9** (1956), 57.
49. *Résultats extraits d'un ouvrage intitulé: De la richesse territoriale du royaume de France* (Paris, 1791). Together with other of Lavoisier's economic writings this is printed in G. Schelle and E. Grimaux, *Lavoisier—statique agricole et projets de réformes* (Paris, 1894). See also *Oeuvres de Lavoisier,* VI, 403–463.
50. The letter was published by René Fric in the *Bulletin historique et scientifique de l'Auvergne, publié par l'Académie des Sciences, Belles-Lettres et Arts de Clermont-Ferrand,* 2nd ser., no. 9 (1924), 145–152. An English translation, inaccurate and misleading, was published by Edgar Fahs Smith in *Old Chemistries* (New York, 1927), pp. 31–32. In a letter to Louis XVI, declining the post of minister of public contributions, Lavoisier wrote in 1792: "I am neither a Jacobin nor a Feuillant; I belong to no political society or club. Accustomed to weigh everything according to my conscience and my reason, I would never have consented to give up my opinions for those of any party." The Feuillants were the moderate constitutionalists whose opinions Lavoisier generally shared, and whose club met in what had been the monastery of the religious order of the Feuillants. This letter, of which a copy survives in the Archives of

the Academy of Sciences (Dossiers Lavoisier, No. 1725), was first published by François Guizot in his *Mélanges biographiques et littéraires* (Paris, 1880), pp. 77–79, where it appears in his article on Lavoisier's widow, entitled "La Comtesse de Rumford." Benjamin Franklin's letters to Lavoisier's colleague in the Academy of Sciences, J. B. Le Roy (13 November 1789), and to David Hartley (4 December 1789) show his deep concern over events in France and an attitude not far different from that of Lavoisier. See Albert Henry Smyth, *The Writings of Benjamin Franklin*, X (1907), pp. 68–69 and 72.

51. For Lavoisier's role in the attempts to reform the Academy, and the political struggles within that body, see Roger Hahn, *The Anatomy of a Scientific Institution* (Berkeley–Los Angeles, 1971), especially chapters 8 and 9.

52. J. Guillaume, "Un mot légendaire: 'La République n'a pas besoin de savants,'" in *Révolution française*, **38** (1900), 385–399, and *Études révolutionnaires*, 1st ser. (Paris, 1908), pp. 136–155.

53. The remark was made to the astronomer Jean-Baptiste Delambre, who reports it in his "Notice sur la vie et les ouvrages de M. le Comte J.-L. Lagrange. *Oeuvres de Lagrange,* ed. J. A. Serret, I (1867), p. xl.

54. Denis I. Duveen, "Lavoisier writes to his wife from prison," *Manuscripts*, **10** (1958), 38–39. The letter is now in the Lavoisier Collection in the Olin Library, Cornell University.

Bibliography

I. ORIGINAL WORKS. For a bibliography of Lavoisier's papers—academic, scientific, and in popular periodicals—and his major and minor separate works, consult Denis I. Duveen and Herbert S. Klickstein, *A Bibliography of the Works of Antoine Laurent Lavoisier, 1743–1794* (London, 1954), and Duveen's *Supplement* (London, 1965).

Lavoisier's published articles, some hitherto unpublished papers, and two of his major books are printed in *Oeuvres de Lavoisier*, 6 vols. (Paris, 1862–1893). The first 4 vols. were edited by the distinguished chemist J. B. Dumas, the last 2 vols. by Edouard Grimaux, Lavoisier's principal biographer. Much, but by no means all, of Lavoisier's surviving correspondence through 1783 has appeared in *Oeuvres de Lavoisier—Correspondance*, 3 fascs. (Paris, 1955–1964), edited by the late René Fric under the auspices of the Académie des Sciences. A further fasc. completed before the death of M. Fric is due to appear. The editing of this work leaves much to be desired; many letters, some quite important, have been overlooked; for a scathing appraisal of fasc. I, see A. Birembaut, "La correspondance de Lavoisier," in *Annales historiques de la Révolution française*, **29** (Oct.–Dec. 1957), 340–351.

Lavoisier's major books are four in number. His *Opuscules physiques et chimiques* (Paris, 1774) was intended to be the first of a series of vols. containing the results of his investigations. The later vols. never materialized. A posthumous reissue of the 1st ed. was published in 1801; the *Opuscules* was trans. with notes and an appendix by Thomas Henry as *Essays Physical and Chemical* (London, 1776). A German trans. by C. E. Weigel appeared as vol. I of his 5-vol. collection entitled *Lavoisier physikalisch-chemische Schriften* (Greifswald, 1783–1794). The remaining 4 vols. contain German versions of a number of Lavoisier's scientific papers (the last 2 vols. were the work of H. F. Link).

Méthode de nomenclature chimique, proposée par MM. de Morveau, Lavoisier, Bertholet [sic] & de Fourcroy. On y a joint un nouveau système de caractères chimiques, adaptés à cette nomenclature, par MM. Hassenfratz & Adet (Paris, 1787). There is a 2nd printing of this 1st ed.; the 2nd ed. appeared in 1789, as vol. III of the 2nd ed. of Lavoisier's *Traité élémentaire de chimie*. It is entitled *Nomenclature chimique, ou synonymie ancienne et moderne, pour servir à l'intelligence des auteurs*. There is an English trans. of this collaborative work by James St. John (London, 1788); an Italian version by Pietro Calloud (Venice, 1790); and a German trans. by Karl von Meidinger (Vienna, 1793). Various abridgments and tabular versions of the new nomenclature. appeared in English, German, and Italian. The chief agent for transmitting the new chemistry to Germany was Christoph Girtanner (1760–1800), who in 1791 brought out a German version of the *Nomenclature chimique* and the next year his *Anfangsgründe der antiphlogistischen Chemie* (Berlin, 1792). For the reception of Lavoisier's work in Italy, see Icilio Guareschi, "Lavoisier, sua vita e sue opere," in *Supplemento annuale alla Enciclo-pedia di chimica scientifica e industriale*, **19** (Turin, 1903), 307–469, esp. 452–455.

In 1778 Lavoisier proposed to devote a 2nd vol. of his *Opuscules* to setting forth a *système général* of chemistry expounded in a rational and deductive fashion, according to the *méthode des géomètres*. Such a work was never written; but this method was used in his most famous book, the *Traité élémentaire de chimie* (Paris, 1789), a book that in fact grew out of the work on the chemical nomenclature and first appeared in a single volume; a 2nd printing in 2 vols. appeared in the same year, as did a 2nd ed. An influential English trans. by Robert Kerr appeared as *Elements of Chemistry, in a New Systematic Order, Containing All the Modern Discoveries* (Edinburgh, 1790). There are several later eds. of Kerr's trans. The *Traité* appeared in German, translated by S. F. Hermbstadt (Berlin–Stettin, 1792); in Dutch, by N. C. de Fremery (Utrecht, 1800); in Italian, by Vincenzo Dandolo (Venice, 1791); and in Spanish, by Juan Manuel Munarriz (Madrid, 1798).

About 1792 Lavoisier planned a complete ed. of his memoirs in 8 vols.; also to be included were papers by some of his disciples. The posthumous *Mémoires de chimie*, printed in 2 vols. for Mme Lavoisier from incomplete proofs partially corrected by Lavoisier, is all that resulted from this project. The vols. are undated (there are no title pages, only half titles), and they were not commercially published; Mme Lavoisier presented copies to selected institutions and individuals. Although Duveen assigns the year 1805 to this work, it was circulating two years earlier—when, as J. R. Partington has shown, Berthollet quoted it by vol. and pg. The *Mémoires*, not repr. in the *Oeuvres*, includes reprints and revisions of previously published papers, as well as hitherto unpublished results, such as experiments carried out toward the close of his collaboration with Laplace in 1783–1784 on problems related to heat. There are several papers by Lavoisier's latter-day collaborator, Armand Seguin.

The chief repository of Lavoisier manuscripts is the Académie des Sciences in Paris, in whose archives one can consult Lavoisier's laboratory notebooks and some twenty *cartons* containing drafts of scientific papers, academy reports, and so on. There are important letters in the Collection de Chazelles in the city library of Clermont-Ferrand, and other manuscripts, notably letters, in the possession of Count Guy de Chabrol. Microfilms of the letters and other documents in the Fonds Chabrol are available in the archives of the Académie des Sciences, as is also a xerographic copy of the second laboratory notebook *(registre)* for the period 9 September 1773 to 5 March 1774. This had been given by François Arago to the library of Perpignan, and for a time was believed lost. See the *Comptes rendus des séances de l'Académie des sciences*, **135** (1902), 549–557 and 574–575. There are scattered documents in various provincial libraries in France, notably Orléans, and important material in the Archives Nationales, chiefly dealing with the period of the Revolution. The Bibliothèque Nationale has little to offer, except Fr. nouv. acq. 5153, which is an account of Lavoisier's repetition of his classic early experiments before an Academy committee. The Lavoisier Collection in the Olin Library of Cornell University was originally assembled by Denis I. Duveen. Besides a number of manuscripts, many books from Lavoisier's own library with his *ex libris*, this includes the most nearly complete assemblage of the books and pamphlets published by Lavoisier, and in nearly all the known editions and variants.

II. SECONDARY LITERATURE. The earliest biographical sketches of Lavoisier appeared in the early days of the Directory: Joseph Jérôme Lalande, "Notice sur la vie et les ouvrages de Lavoisier," in *Magasin encyclopédique*, **5** (1795), 174–188, English trans. in *Philosophical Magazine*, **9** (1801), 78–85; and Antoine François de Fourcroy, *Notice sur la vie et les travaux de Lavoisier* (Paris, 1796). Other early sketches are Thomas Thomson, "Biographical Account of M. Lavoisier," in *Annals of Philosophy*, **2** (1813), 81–92; and Georges Cuvier, "Lavoisier," in L. G. Michaud, ed., *Biographie universelle*, new ed. (Paris, 1854–1865), XXIII, 414–418, based in part on information, much of it inaccurate, supplied by Lavoisier's widow. See Charles C. Gillispie, "Notice biographique de Lavoisier par Madame Lavoisier," in *Revue d'histoire des sciences et de leurs applications*, **9** (1956), 52–61. The standard biography is Edouard Grimaux, *Lavoisier 1743–1795, d'après sa correspondance, ses manuscrits, ses papiers de famille et d'autres documents inédits* (Paris, 1888; 2nd ed., 1896; 3rd ed., 1899). No trans. was ever published, and most subsequent biographies have relied heavily upon Grimaux—for example, Mary Louise Foster, *Life of*

147

Lavoisier (Northampton, Mass., 1926); J. A. Cochrane, *Lavoisier* (London, 1931); and Douglas McKie, *Antoine Lavoisier* (London–New York, 1952). For a general appraisal of this literature, see Henry Guerlac, "Lavoisier and His Biographers," in *Isis,* **45** (1954), 51–62. The well-documented study by R. Dujarric de la Rivière and Madeleine Chabrier, *La vie et l'oeuvre de Lavoisier* (Paris, 1959), is most useful for the nonscientific aspects of Lavoisier's career. A readable study, which makes use of some recent research, is Léon Velluz, *Vie de Lavoisier* (Paris, 1966). Unfortunately, although there is a list of published sources, the text itself is not documented. Short but informative is Lucien Scheler, *Lavoisier et le principe chimique* (Paris, 1964). Y. G. Dorfman's *Lavoisier* (Moscow, 1962) is a scholarly and comprehensive book accessible to readers of Russian. Regrettably, there is no evidence that the portrait supposed to represent Lavoisier ca. 1778–1779, reproduced opposite page 136, is authentic.

There have been a number of general investigations of Lavoisier's work in chemistry. The pioneer study is surely the IVe Leçon of J.-B. Dumas, *Leçons sur la philosophie chimique professées au Collège de France* (Paris, n.d., but certainly 1836, the year the lectures were delivered). A second edition, an unaltered reprint, appeared in 1878. Still valuable, especially for its excerpts and paraphrases from Lavoisier's laboratory notebooks, is Marcelin Berthelot, *La révolution chimique—Lavoisier* (Paris, 1890, 2nd ed., 1902). Douglas McKie, *Antoine Lavoisier, the Father of Modern Chemistry* (Philadelphia, 1935), owes

148

much to the pioneer work of Andrew Norman Meldrum (see below). In the same year appeared Hélène Metzger's classic *La philosophie de la matière chez Lavoisier* (Paris, 1935). Worth consulting is Sir Harold Hartley, "Antoine Laurent Lavoisier, 26 August 1743–8 May 1794," in *Proceedings of the Royal Society*, **189A** (1947), 427–456. Extremely valuable for the use made of the *procès-verbaux* of the Academy of Sciences and other unpublished documents relating to Lavoisier's work is Maurice Daumas, *Lavoisier, théoricien et expérimentateur* (Paris, 1955). An elaborate treatment of Lavoisier's achievements is given by J. R. Partington, *A History of Chemistry*, III, ch. IX. A general review of the state of Lavoisier studies is given by W. A. Smeaton, "New Light on Lavoisier: The Research of the Last Ten Years," in *History of Science*, **2** (1963), 51–69.

For eighteenth-century chemical theory before Lavoisier the classic studies are Hélène Metzger, *Les Doctrines chimiques en France du début du XVIIᵉ à la fin du XVIIIᵉ siècle* (Paris, 1923) and her *Newton, Stahl, Boerhaave et la doctrine chimique* (Paris, 1930). The technological background is described in Henry Guerlac, "Some French Antecedents of the Chemical Revolution," in *Chymia*, **5** (1959), 73–112. For Lavoisier's teacher of chemistry, see Rhoda Rappaport, "G. F. Rouelle: An Eighteenth-Century Chemist and Teacher," *ibid.*, **6** (1960), 68–101, and her "Rouelle and Stahl—The Phlogistic Revolution in France," *ibid.*, **7** (1961), 73–102. A different emphasis is found in Martin Fichman, "French Stahlism and Chemical Studies of Air, 1750–1779," in *Ambix*, **18** (1971), 94–122.

Studies of special aspects of Lavoisier's chemical research

abound. For the early stages of his career, see A. N. Meldrum, "Lavoisier's Early Work on Science, 1763–1771," in *Isis*, **19** (1933), 330–363; **20** (1934), 396–425; and his "Lavoisier's Work on the Nature of Water and the Supposed Transmutation of Water Into Earth (1768–1773)," in *Archeion*, **14** (1932), 246–247. These studies have been corrected or amplified by Henry Guerlac, "A Note on Lavoisier's Scientific Education," in *Isis*, **47** (1956), 211–216; by Rhoda Rappaport, "Lavoisier's Geologic Activities, 1763–1792," *ibid.*, **58** (1968), 375–384; and by J. B. Gough, "Lavoisier's Early Career in Science, an Examination of Some New Evidence," in *British Journal for the History of Science*, **4** (1968), 52–57, who was the first to identify (correcting Daumas) Lavoisier's notes from Eller and to see their significance for Lavoisier's theory of heat and vaporization. Consult also W. A. Smeaton, *"L'avant-coureur*, the Journal in Which Some of Lavoisier's Earliest Research Was Reported," in *Annals of Science*, **13** (1957), 219–234. This article actually appeared in 1959. There is useful information in E. McDonald, "The Collaboration of Bucquet and Lavoisier," in *Ambix*, **13** (1966), 74–84.

For Lavoisier's first experiments on combustion, the pioneer work of A. N. Meldrum, *The Eighteenth Century Revolution in Science—The First Phase* (Calcutta–London–New York, n.d. [1930]), is classic. See too his "Lavoisier's Three Notes on Combustion: 1772," in *Archeion*, **14** (1932), 15–30; also Max Speter, "Die entdeckte Lavoisier-Note vom 20 Oktober 1772," in *Zeitschrift für angewandte Chemie*, **45** (1932); his "Kritisches über die Entstehung von Lavoisiers System," *ibid.*, **39** (1926), 578–582; and his article "Lavoisier," in Gunther Bugge, ed., *Das Buch der grossen Chemiker* (Berlin, 1929), I, 304–333. For new light on the famous sealed note, see Henry Guerlac, "A Curious Lavoisier Episode," in *Chymia*, 7 (1961), 103–108. For the research leading up to Lavoisier's investigations in the autumn of 1772, see Guerlac, *Lavoisier—The Crucial Year* (Ithaca, N.Y., 1961), where the basic documents are reproduced in the app. For a reassessment see Robert E. Kohler, Jr., "The Origin of Lavoisier's First Experiments on Combustion," in *Isis*, 63 (1972), 349–355. The discovery of oxygen, and the influence of Priestley upon Lavoisier, are treated by Meldrum, *Eighteenth Century Revolution in Science*, chap. 5; by Sir Philip Hartog, "The Newer Views of Priestley and Lavoisier," in *Annals of Science*, 5 (1941), 1–56; and by Sidney J. French, "The Chemical Revolution—The Second Phase," in *Journal of Chemical Education*, 27 (1950), 83–88. C. E. Perrin, "Prelude to Lavoisier's Theory of Calcination—Some Observations on Mercurius Calcinatus per se," in *Ambix*, 16 (1969), 140–151, casts new light on Lavoisier's possible debt to Priestley and to Pierre Bayen.

For the stages in the preparation of Lavoisier's most famous book see Maurice Daumas, "L'élaboration du *Traité de Chimie* de Lavoisier," in *Archives internationales d'histoire des sciences*, 29 (1950), 570–590. For Lavoisier's attitude towards affinity theories see Daumas, "Les conceptions sur les affinités chimiques et la constitution de la matière," in *Thalès* (1949–1950), 69–80. Both these papers discuss unpublished notes for a work Lavoisier did not live to undertake seriously, to be entitled "Cours de chimie

expérimentale" or "Cours de philosophie expérimentale."
A provocative paper on the famous "Discours préliminaire" is Robert Delhez, "Révolution chimique et Révolution française: *Le Discours préliminaire* au *Traité élémentaire de chimie* de Lavoisier," in *Revue des questions scientifiques*, **143** (1972), 3–26.

Lavoisier's early theory of the elements and of the aeriform state of matter has been the focus of recent investigations. Guerlac, in "A Lost Memoir of Lavoisier," in *Isis*,
50 (1959), 125–129, attempts to reconstruct the character
of a supposedly lost memoir by Lavoisier. This document
was published with other *inédits* by René Fric, "Contribution à l'étude de l'évolution des idées de Lavoisier sur la
nature de l'air et sur la calcination des métaux," in *Archives
internationales d'histoire des sciences*, **12** (1959); 125–129,
actually published 1960. Further contributions are Maurice
Crosland, "The Development of the Concept of the
Gaseous State as a Third State of Matter," in *Proceedings
of the 10th International Congress of the History of Science*
II (Paris, 1962), 851–854; J. B. Gough, "Nouvelle contribution à l'étude de l'évolution des idées de Lavoisier sur la
nature de l'air et sur la calcination des métaux," in
Archives internationales d'histoire des sciences, **22** (1969),
267–275, publishes a draft by Lavoisier entitled "De l'élas-
ticité et de la formation des fluides élastiques," dated end
of Feb. 1775. See also Robert Siegfried, "Lavoisier's View
of the Gaseous State and Its Early Application to Pneumatic Chemistry," in *Isis*, **63** (1972), 59–78. The most extensive treatment of this aspect of Lavoisier's work is Gough's
Ph.D. dissertation, "The Foundations of Modern Chemistry: The Origin and Development of the Concept of the

Gaseous State and Its Role in the Chemical Revolution of the Eighteenth Century" (Cornell University, June 1971). Robert J. Morris has criticized, with some justice, Guerlac's narrow interpretation of Lavoisier's "Système sur les élémens" of the summer of 1772 but denies that it was in fact a system of the elements. See R. J. Morris, "Lavoisier on Air and Fire: The Memoir of July 1772," in *Isis*, **60** (1969), 374–377; and Guerlac's reply, *ibid.*, 381–382.

Closely related to the problem of the aeriform state is Lavoisier's caloric theory, a matter discussed cursorily in most accounts of his work. But recent work has reopened the question. Henry Guerlac, "Laplace's Collaboration With Lavoisier," in *Actes du XIIᵉ Congrès international d'histoire des sciences; Paris, 1968*, III B (Paris, 1971), 31–36, is an abstract of a forthcoming study of the collaborative experiments of Lavoisier and Laplace on heat. Robert Fox, *The Caloric Theory of Gases, From Lavoisier to Regnault* (Oxford, 1971), has a long first chapter entitled "The Study of Gases and Heat to 1800." An important study is Robert J. Morris, "Lavoisier and the Caloric Theory," in *British Journal for the History of Science*, **6** (1972), 1–38.

For Lavoisier's instrument makers see Maurice Daumas, *Les instruments scientifiques aux XVIIᵉ et XVIIIᵉ siècles* (Paris, 1953). Descriptions of surviving pieces of Lavoisier's apparatus are given in P. Truchot, "Les instruments de Lavoisier. Relation d'une visite à La Canière (Puy-de-Dôme) où se trouve réunis les appareils ayant servi à Lavoisier," in *Annales de chimie et de physique*, 5th ser., **18** (1879), 289–319; also Maurice Daumas, "Les appareils d'expérimentation de Lavoisier," in *Chymia*, **3** (1950), 45–

62; and chs. 5 and 6 of Daumas, *Lavoisier, théoricien et expérimentateur*; and Graham Luske, "Mementoes of Lavoisier, Notes on a Trip to Château de la Canière," in *Journal of the American Medical Association*, **85** (1925), 1246–1247. An attempt to evaluate the quantitative precision of Lavoisier's experiments is made by M. Guichard, *Essai historique sur les mesures en chimie* (Paris, 1937), 53–72.

On the synthesis and decomposition of water, the fullest account is in J. R. Partington, *History of Chemistry*, III, 325–338, 436–456. Maurice Daumas and Denis Duveen, "Lavoisier's Relatively Unknown Large-Scale Decomposition and Synthesis of Water, February 27 and 28, 1785," in *Chymia*, **5** (1959), 113–129, discuss in detail the experiments of Meusnier and Lavoisier that were never formally published, and were described only in the account printed in the obscure *Journal polytype des sciences et des arts* of 26 Feb. 1786; repr. in *Oeuvres de Lavoisier*, V, 320–339. C. E. Perrin, in a note entitled "Lavoisier, Monge and the Synthesis of Water," *British Journal for the History of Science*, **6** (1973), 424–428, accounts for the apparent coincidence of the synthesis of water by Lavoisier and Laplace and by Gaspard Monge in the summer of 1783 by suggesting a knowledge (prior to the disclosure by Blagden of Cavendish's results) of Priestley's repetition of Cavendish's experiment.

For the pioneer balloon experiments, the most elaborate contemporary source is Barthélemy Faujas de Saint-Fond, *Description des expériences de la machine aérostatique de MM. Montgolfier ... suivie de mémoires sur le gaz inflam-*

mable etc., 2 vols. (Paris, 1783–1784). Gaston Tissandier, *Histoire des ballons et des aéronautes célèbres* (Paris, 1887), is an admirable account, superbly illustrated. The report of the first commission on the Montgolfier balloons (composed of Le Roy, Tillet, Brisson, Cadet de Gassicourt, Lavoisier, Bossut, Condorcet, and Desmarest) appeared first as a pamphlet in 1784 and later in the *Mémoires* of the Academy of Sciences. It is repr. in *Oeuvres de Lavoisier*, III, 719–735, and in *Extraits des mémoires de Lavoisier concernant la météorologie et l'aéronautique* (Paris, 1926), published by the Office National Météorologique de France.

A brief account of Lavoisier's work on organic analysis is given in Ferenc Szabadváry, *History of Analytical Chemistry* (Oxford–London, 1966), pp. 284–287. His studies of alcoholic fermentation are described in P. Schutzenberger, *Les fermentations*, 5th ed. (Paris, 1889), pp. 14–15; Carl Oppenheimer, *Ferments and Their Actions*, trans. from the German by C. Ainsworth Mitchell (London, 1901), pp. 3–4; and Arthur Harden, *Alcoholic Fermentation* (London, 1911), pp. 2–3.

For Lavoisier's geology see Pierre Comte, "Aperçu sur l'oeuvre géologique de Lavoisier," in *Annales de la Société géologique du Nord*, **69** (1949), 369–375; A. V. Carozzi, "Lavoisier's Fundamental Contribution to Stratigraphy," in *Ohio Journal of Science*, **65** (1965), 71–85; Rhoda Rappaport, "The Early Disputes Between Lavoisier and Monnet, 1777–1781," in *British Journal for the History of Science*, **4** (1969), 233–244; "Lavoisier's Geologic Activities, 1763–1792," in *Isis*, **58** (1968), 375–384; "The Geolog-

ical Atlas of Guettard, Lavoisier, and Monnet," in Cecil
J. Schneer, ed., *Towards a History of Geology* (Cambridge,
Mass., 1969), pp. 272–287; and "Lavoisier's Theory of the
Earth," to appear in *British Journal for the History of
Science*.

On the new nomenclature, see M. P. Crosland, *Historical
Studies in the Language of Chemistry* (London, 1962),
chs. 3–8. See also Denis I. Duveen and Herbert S. Klickstein, "The Introduction of Lavoisier's Chemical Nomenclature Into America," in *Isis*, **45** (1954), 278–292, 368–
382; and H. M. Leicester, "The Spread of the Theory of
Lavoisier in Russia," in *Chymia*, **5** (1959), 138–144. For
Britain and Germany, see Crosland, *Historical Studies . . .*,
pp. 193–206, 207–210.

Lavoisier's physiological writings, notably on respiration, are discussed in Charles Richet, "Lavoisier et la
chaleur animale," in *Revue scientifique*, **34** (1884), 141–
146; Alphonse Milne-Edwards, *Notice sur les travaux
physiologiques de Lavoisier* (Paris, 1885); G. Masson, ed.,
Lavoisier, la chaleur et la respiration, 1770–1789 (Paris,
1892); M. J. Rosenthal, "Lavoisier et son influence sur les
progrès de la physiologie," in *Revue scientifique*, **47** (1891),
33–42; J. C. Hemmeter, "Lavoisier and the History of the
Physiology of Respiration and Metabolism," in *Johns
Hopkins Hospital Bulletin*, **29** (1918), 254–264; Graham
Lusk, "A History of Metabolism," in L. F. Barker, ed.,
Endocrinology and Metabolism (New York, 1922), III,
3–78—a section of this history is devoted to Lavoisier,
pp. 19–30; R. Foregger, "Respiration Experiments of
Lavoisier," in *Archives internationales d'histoire des
sciences*, **13** (1960), 103–106; and Everett Mendelsohn,

Heat and Life (Cambridge, Mass., 1964), 134–139, 146–165, which discusses Lavoisier's work perceptively. Charles A. Culotta, "Respiration and the Lavoisier Tradition: Theory and Modification, 1777–1850," in *Transactions of the American Philosophical Society*, n.s. **62** (1972), 3–40, is the most recent study. See also John F. Fulton, Denis I. Duveen, and Herbert S. Klickstein, "Antoine Laurent Lavoisier's Réflexions sur les effets de l'éther nitreux dans l'économie animale," in *Journal of the History of Medicine and Allied Sciences*, **8** (1953), 318–323; W. A. Smeaton, "Lavoisier's Membership of the Société Royale de Médecine," in *Annals of Science*, **12** (1956), 228–244; and Denis I. Duveen and H. S. Klickstein, "Antoine Laurent Lavoisier's Contributions to Medicine and Public Health," in *Bulletin of the History of Medicine*, **29** (1955), 164–179.

For Lavoisier's role in the improvement of saltpeter production and gunpowder manufacture, see Robert P. Multhauf, "The French Crash Program for Saltpeter Production, 1776–94," in *Technology and Culture*, **12** (1971), 163–181, and the important study by Lucien Scheler, "Lavoisier et la régie des poudres," *Revue d'histoire des sciences et de leurs applications*, **26** (1973), 193–222. There is valuable source material on the Régie des Poudres in the La Forte Collection in Cornell's Olin Library. The gunpowder situation in America at the outbreak of the Revolution, and the aid received from France, is described by Orlando W. Stephenson, "The Supply of Gunpowder in 1776," in *American Historical Review*, **30** (1925), 271–281. More than half of vol. V of the *Oeuvres de Lavoisier* is devoted to his papers on saltpeter and the work for the Régie des Poudres. See also J. R. Partington, "Lavoisier's Memoir on the Composition of Nitric Acid," in *Annals of Science*, **9** (1953), 96–98. The relations between Franklin and Lavoisier are described by H. S. van Klooster, "Franklin and Lavoisier," in *Journal of Chemical Education*, **23** (1946), 107–109; and by Denis I. Duveen and H. S. Klickstein, "Benjamin Franklin (1706–1790) and Antoine Laurent Lavoisier (1743–1794)," in *Annals of Science*, **11** (1955), 103–128, 271–302, and **13** (1957), 30–46. See also Claude A. Lopez, "Saltpetre, Tin and Gunpowder: Addenda to the Correspondence of Lavoisier and Franklin," in *Annals of Science*, **16** (1960), 83–94. For a remarkable letter from Lavoisier to Franklin, see René Fric, "Une lettre inédite de Lavoisier à B. Franklin," in *Bulletin historique et scientifique de l'Auvergne*, **9** (1924), 145–152.

On Lavoisier as a financier and economic theorist, there is no general study, although R. Bigo, *La Caisse d'Escompte (1776–1793) et les origines de la Banque de France* (Paris, 1927) may prove helpful. Nor is there a satisfactory investigation of the General Farm, although useful material can be found in Adrien Delahante, *Une famille de finance au XVIIIe siècle*, 2 vols. (Paris, 1880), and a recent ambitious study, Yves Durand, *Les fermiers généraux au XVIIIe siècle* (Paris, 1971), is a substantial contribution. Eugène Daire and Gustave de Molinari, *Mélanges d'économie politique*, I (Paris, 1847), 577–580, contains a "Notice sur Lavoisier," followed by two of his essays in political economy. See also G. Schelle and E. Grimaux, *Lavoisier—*

statistique agricole et projets de réformes (Paris, 1894); and R. Dujarric de la Rivière, *Lavoisier économiste* (Paris, 1949). For Lavoisier's relations with Pierre Samuel Dupont de Nemours and Pierre's son, see Bessie Gardner Du Pont, *Life of Éleuthère Irénée du Pont from Contemporary Correspondence* (11 vols., Newark, Delaware, 1923–1926), *passim*, I, 141–145, and R. Dujarric de la Rivière, *E. I. Du Pont de Nemours, élève de Lavoisier* (Paris, 1954), esp. 157–158.

For Lavoisier's interest in agriculture, see Henri Pigeonneau and Alfred de Foville, *L'administration de l'agriculture au controle générale des finances (1785–1787). Procès-verbaux et rapports* (Paris, 1882); and Louis Passy, *Histoire de la Société nationale d'agriculture de France*, I, *1761–1793* (Paris, 1912), which is all that appeared. André J. Bourde, *The Influence of England on the French Agronomes, 1750–1789* (Cambridge, 1953); and *Agronomie et agronomes en France au XVIIIᵉ siècle*, 3 vols. (Paris, 1967), provide the essential background with incidental references to Lavoisier. See also W. A. Smeaton, "Lavoisier's Membership of the Société Royale d'Agriculture and the Comité d'Agriculture," in *Annals of Science*, **12** (1956), 267–277.

Lavoisier's role as an officer of the Academy of Sciences, before and during the French Revolution, bulks large in Roger Hahn, *The Anatomy of a Scientific Institution, the Paris Academy of Sciences, 1666–1803* (Berkeley–Los Angeles, 1971). See also Lucien Scheler, "Antoine Laurent Lavoisier et Michel Adanson, rédacteurs de programmes des prix à l'Académie des Sciences," *Revue d'histoire des sciences et de leurs applications*, **14** (1961), 257–284. There are glimpses of Lavoisier and his wife in Arthur Young's *Travels in France*, the best (and fully annotated) ed. of which is the French trans. by Henri Sée, *Voyages en France en 1787, 1788 et 1789*, 3 vols. (Paris, 1931), espec. I, pp. 189–191; in Beatrix Cary Davenport, ed., *A Diary of the French. Revolution by Gouverneur Morris, 1752–1816* (Boston, 1939); in V. A. Eyles, "The Evolution of a Chemist, Sir James Hall," in *Annals of Science*, **19** (1963), 153–182; and in J. A. Chaldecott, "Scientific Activities in Paris in 1791," *ibid.*, **24** (1968), 21–52.

Grimaux gives much useful information about Mme Lavoisier, her education, her marriage, and her contributions to her husband's career in his *Lavoisier*, 2nd ed., pp. 35–44; for the genealogy of her family and an account of her life after Lavoisier's execution, see the appendixes to the same work, pp. 330–336. Worth consulting is Denis I. Duveen, "Madame Lavoisier, 1758–1836," in *Chymia*, **4** (1953), 13–29. Mme Lavoisier's major contribution to the campaign for the new chemistry was her (anonymous) trans. of Richard Kirwan's *Essay on Phlogiston* (London, 1784); the French version, *Essai sur le phlogistique* (Paris, 1788), has notes by the translator and extensive critical commentary by Guyton de Morveau, Laplace, Monge, Berthollet, Fourcroy, and Lavoisier himself. Grimaux (*op. cit.*, p. 42) speaks of her "traductions inédites de Priestley, Cavendish, Henry, etc." Her last effort along these lines is her trans. of Kirwan's "Strength of Acids and the Proportion of Ingredients in Neutral

Salts," in *Proceedings of the Royal Irish Academy*, **4** (1790), 3–89. It appeared in *Annales de chimie*, **14** (1792), 152, 211, 238–286.

Lavoisier's role in the French Revolution, his imprisonment, and his execution have produced a substantial, and sometimes controversial, literature. See, for example, Denis I. Duveen, "Antoine Laurent Lavoisier (1743–1794), a Note Regarding His Domicile During the French Revolution," in *Isis*, **42** (1951), 233–234; and "Antoine Laurent Lavoisier and the French Revolution," in *Journal of Chemical Education*, **31** (1954), 60–65; **34** (1957), 502–503; **35** (1958), 233–234, 470–471. See also Marguerite Vergnaud, "Un savant pendant la Révolution," in *Cahiers internationaux de sociologie*, **17** (1954), 123–139; Denis I. Duveen and Marguerite Vergnaud, "L'explication de la mort de Lavoisier," in *Archives internationales d'histoire des sciences*, **9** (1956), 43–50; Denis I. Duveen, "Lavoisier Writes to Fourcroy From Prison," in *Notes and Records. Royal Society of London*, **13** (1958), 59–60; and "Lavoisier Writes to His Wife From Prison," in *Manuscripts*, **10** (fall 1958), 38–39; and Denis I. Duveen and H. S. Klickstein, "Some New Facts Relating to the Arrest of Antoine Laurent Lavoisier," in *Isis*, **49** (1958), 347–348. On the problem of whether Fourcroy interceded on behalf of Lavoisier, see G. Kersaint, "Fourcroy a-t-il fait des démarches pour sauver Lavoisier?" in *Revue générale des sciences pures et appliquées*, **65** (1958), 151–152; and his "Lavoisier, Fourcroy et le scrutin épuratoire du Lycée de la rue de Valois," in *Bulletin. Société chimique de France* (1958), 259. For a comment on Kersaint's article, see

Maurice Daumas, "Justification de l'attitude de Fourcroy pendant la Terreur," in *Revue d'histoire des sciences et de leurs applications,* **11** (1958), 273–274.

Other aspects of Lavoisier's career during the Revolution are mentioned by Henry Guerlac, "Some Aspects of Science During the French Revolution," in *Scientific Monthly,* **80** (1955), 93–101, repr. in Philipp G. Frank, ed., *The Validation of Scientific Theories* (Boston, 1957), 171–191; J. Guillaume, "Lavoisier anti-clérical et révolutionnaire," in *Révolution française,* **26** (1907), 403–423, repr. in *Études révolutionnaires,* 1st ser. (Paris, 1908), 354–379; Lucien Scheler, *Lavoisier et la Révolution française. II. Le journal de Fourgeroux de Bondaroy* (Paris, 1960), ed. with the collaboration of W. A. Smeaton. See also Smeaton's "The Early Years of the Lycée and the Lycée des Arts. A Chapter in the Lives of A. L. Lavoisier and A. F. de Fourcroy," in *Annals of Science,* **11** (1955), 257–267; **12** (1956), 267–277; and his "Lavoisier's Membership of the Assembly of Representatives of the Commune of Paris, 1789–1790," *ibid.,* **13** (1957), 235–248. For the text of letters seized at Lavoisier's house on 10 and 11 Sept. 1793, see Douglas McKie, "Antoine Laurent Lavoisier, F.R.S.," in *Notes and Records of the Royal Society,* **7** (1949), 1–41.

For the educational proposals attributed to Lavoisier, see Harold J. Abrahams, "Lavoisier's Proposals for French Education," in *Journal of Chemical Education,* **31** (1954), 413–416; and his "Summary of Lavoisier's Proposals for Training in Science and Medicine," in *Bulletin of the History of Medicine,* **32** (1958), 389–407. That Lavoisier was by no means the sole author of the *Réflexions sur l'instruction publique* has been shown by K. M. Baker and W. A. Smeaton, "The Origins and Authorship of the Educational Proposals Published in 1793 by the *Bureau de Consultation des Arts et Métiers* and Generally Ascribed to Lavoisier," in *Annals of Science*, **21** (1965), 33–46.

Illustration Credits

Pages 13, 15 (top), 22, 25, 34 (photograph by H. Roger-Viollet): Originals in author's collection

Pages 14, 28: Courtesy Historic Urban Plans, Ithaca, N.Y.

Page 15 (bottom): Courtesy Musée de la Ville d'Etampes

Page 16: Courtesy Muséum National d'Histoire Naturelle, Paris

Page 17: Oeuvres de Lavoisier (Paris, 1862-1893), vol. V, plate 1

Pages 18, 26, 29, 36, 38, 42, 43, 44: Courtesy Cornell University Library

Pages 19, 20, 21, 23, 35: Courtesy Bibliothèque Nationale, Paris

Page 24: Stephen Hales, *Vegetable Staticks* (London, 1727)

Pages 27, 30, 40, 41: Edouard Grimaux, *Lavoisier,* 3rd ed. (Paris, 1899)

Page 31: Collection, The Rockefeller University

Page 32: Antoine-Laurent Lavoisier, *Traité élémentaire de chimie* (Paris, 1789), plate VI

Pages 33 (bottom), 37 (top and bottom): Courtesy Musée des Techniques, Conservatoire des Arts et Métiers, Paris

Page 39: Courtesy National Library of Medicine, Bethesda, Md.

Index

Academy of Amiens, 65
Academy of Sciences (Paris), 59, 60, 61,
    62, 63-64, 66, 67, 68, 69, 80, 81, 82,
    83, 85, 86, 91, 92, 96, 97, 98, 100,
    103, 104, 106, 121, 122, 124, 128, 129
    Committee of Improving Balloons,
        100, 101
    Histoire et mémoires, 69-70, 85, 86, 98,
        104
    Mémoires des savants étrangers, 59
acetic radical, 115
acid, acetic, 94
    product of fermentation, 119
acid, carbonic, 94
acid, muriatic (hydrochloric), 94
acid, nitric, 91, 92, 94
acid, oxalic, 94
acid, phosphoric, 90, 92
acid, sulphuric (vitriolic), 58, 89, 92, 93,
    94
    air in composition of, 92
acidifiable principle, 91, 92
acids
    constitution of, 87, 88-89, 90, 91
    oxygen theory of, 92, 94, 116-117
acidum pingue, 89, 90
Adet, Pierre-Auguste, 109
Advisory Bureau for the Arts and Trades
    *(Bureau de Consultation des Arts
    et Métiers),* 127
aerial acid (Bergman), 89
aerial fluid or gas, 71, 90, 93
aeriform fluids, 74, 80, 87, 95, 103
aerostats, *see* balloons
affinity, tables of, 114
Agricola, Georgius, *De re metallica*
    (1556), 62

air
    atmospheric, not a simple substance,
        75
    better than common air (oxygen), 92
    dephlogisticated (oxygen), 85, 86, 91,
        97, 120-121
    elasticity of, 70, 80
    eminently respirable (oxygen), 87, 92,
        93, 121
    fixation of, 72; *see also* fixed air
    inflammable (hydrogen), 79, 90, 95,
        97, 100, 101, 108; *see also*
        hydrogen
    J. T. Eller on, 70
    role in combustion and calcination, 80
    vital, *see* vital air
air nitreux (nitric oxide), 91
air pump, use of, 71, 103
Alaterre, Jean d', 64
alcohol, 73, 103
    product of fermentation, 118
Alembert, Jean Le Rond d', 48, 49, 74,
    113
    Traité de dynamique, 48, 113
alkaline earths, 108
alkalis, 108, 115
    causticity of, 77
Alsace and Lorraine, 55
American Philosophical Society, 110
Amiens, 65
ammonia, Berthollet's analysis of, 115,
    117
Ancien Régime, 125
animal heat, measurement of, 104, 122
animal magnetism, 125
Annales de chimie, 109
antiphlogistic chemistry, 76

167

INDEX

nitrogen (*azote* or *mofette atmosphérique*), 92, 108, 115, 117
nitrous air (nitric oxide), 84, 85, 91, 92
Normandy, 54

Observations sur la physique, sur l'histoire naturelle et sur les arts (Rozier's Journal), 70, 85, 98, 106
organic acids, 94
organic compounds, combustion analysis of, 117, 118
organic radicals, 108, 115
Orge River, 66
oxyacids, 76, 94
oxygen, 47, 76, 83, 87, 94, 95, 96, 108, 115-116, 117, 118, 121, 122, 123
absorption by the blood, 122
active agent in combustion and calcination, 76
constituent of organic substances, 118
role in respiration, 122, 123
oxygen principle (*principe oxigine*), 93, 98, 102, 105

Paracelsus, *tria prima*, 116
Paris
Arsenal of, Lavoisier's laboratory and residence, 66, 101
Astronomical Observatory, cellars of, 63
Commune of, 126
customs duties entering, 64
Lavoisier's long absence from, 55
Parlement of, 48
Place de la Révolution, 130
prisons and hospitals of, 125
street lighting of, 60
water supply of, 66
Paulze, Jacques, 65, 130
Paulze, Marie-Anne-Pierrette, *see* Lavoisier, Madame
pelagic beds, 56
pelican, 68. 69
pelican, 68, 69
philosophes, 125
phlogiston, 75, 76, 83, 85, 105, 111

theory of combustion, 76, 85, 103
Lavoisier's open attack upon, 104, 105
phosphoric acid, composition of, 90, 91, 92
phosphorus, 108
absorption of air by, 79, 81, 90
combustion of, 79, 92
element or *substance simple*, 116
physics, experimental, (*physique expérimentale*), 48, 61
physiocrats, 125
physique générale, class of in Academy, 61
Picardy, 65
Pierrefonds, 48
Pilatre de Rozier, Jean-François, 99
plaster of Paris, 58, 59
platinum, melting of in carbon-oxygen flame, 96
pleasure-pain principle, 113
pneumatic chest or gasholder (*caisse pneumatique*), 95, 96
redesign of, 101
pneumatic trough, 102
potable waters, analysis of, 63
potash, 115
Pott, J.H., 58
Priestley, Joseph, 61, 76, 78, 84, 85, 86, 87, 91, 97, 105, 106, 120
Directions for Impregnating Water with Fixed Air (1772), 78
Experiments and Observations on Different Kinds of Air, (1774-5-7), 78, 85
on gaseous exchange of plants, 78
prepares oxygen gas, 83-84, 85
repeats experiment of Cavendish, 97
Provincial Assembly of Orléanais, 125
Punctis, Constance, 49
Punctis, Emilie, 49

quicklime, 89
causticity of, 77

Reign of Terror, 47, 129
respiration, chemistry of, 120, 121

173